26MALTS
SOME JOY RIDE

EDITED BY **STUART DELVES, JAMIE JAUNCEY & DAMIAN MULLAN**

First published in Great Britain in 2005 by
Cyan Books, an imprint of

Cyan Communications Limited
119 Wardour Street
London W1F 0UW
United Kingdom
www.cyanbooks.com

A CIP record for this book is available from
the British Library

ISBN 1-904879-61-6

Book design by So... *www.soitbegins.co.uk*
Photography by Niall Hendrie

Printed in Great Britain by
Cambrian Printers, Aberystwyth

Bound in Great Britain by
TJ International, Padstow, Cornwall

CONTENTS

FOREWORD

The Scotch Malt Whisky Society began in the 1970s when a group of friends clubbed together to buy and share a single cask of the finest malt whisky. To this day everything the Society does is based on the influence and individuality of the single cask.

The individuality of the single cask malt and the responses it provokes lie at the heart of the Society's relationship with its members and is the inspiration behind the 26 Malts project.

Every cask matures its contents in a different way. No two casks are exactly the same. They might be filled on the same day with the same new spirit but after many years maturation, even lying side by side, each cask will have exerted its own influence on the contents under its care.

That unique influence is reflected in the colour, texture, aroma, taste and aftertaste of the spirit it yields when bottled at cask strength. What's more the response and reaction of each person tasting the malt is as unique as the cask itself.

What better inspiration for a creative project that brings together the UK's finest writers and graphic designers? And what better mechanism to express this creativity than the bottle label?

As part of the creative brief we immersed the teams in the Society and held introductory tastings to inspire and equip them for the task in hand. The designs that follow demonstrate how the Society's malt whisky has fired the imagination and how creativity can cross all sorts of boundaries to inspire and entertain as we discover new avenues of creative expression and interpretation.

From the moment the Society committed to this ambitious project, we knew that it would challenge as well as inspire. It is to the credit of both the project team and all the creative teams involved that **26 Malts** has arrived and we are delighted and excited at the diversity of language, imagery, colour and sheer creativity this project has provoked.

CHARLOTTE HALLIDAY
Marketing Manager
The Scotch Malt Whisky Society

THE ANGEL'S SHARE
STUART DELVES & JAMIE JAUNCEY ON HOW THE PROJECT CAME ABOUT

SD: *26 Malts* – how did it all start? Where does anything start? Tracing back there are always seeds within seeds. Reading and then meeting John Simmons is a good place to stick in the pin. (Yes, it's all his fault.) I first met John in November 2002 when he was Verbal Identity Director at Interbrand. We sat in a quiet room above The Strand. I recall huge white leather armchairs and talking about creativity in the workplace, poetry and Riddley Walker, the connection man in Russell Hoban's novel, trying, and brilliantly succeeding, to make sense of a post-atomised world in a broken down and broken up language.

I offered John two things: to come and talk at the Edinburgh International Book Festival (my new company Henzteeth would sponsor the event) and co-tutor the first ever Creative Writing for Business course in partnership with the Arvon Foundation (for whom I used to work as a Centre Director). After all, his first publication *Telling Stories* had articulated and confirmed everything I believed about writing for business – that storytelling was the key to this mostly straitjacketed genre. It was something I had come to experience, with tremendous professional satisfaction, writing for the Scotch Whisky industry on brands like Highland Park and Black Bottle. I wanted to offer John something in return.

John accepted. Both invitations were fulfilled. In fact, they've spawned sequels. And there was another connection. Jamie Jauncey chaired the Book Festival event. Another Simmons fan. And now a friend. When John left Interbrand in the autumn of 2003 and, amongst other things, set up 26, Jamie and I joined up and talked about creating a Scottish chapter. We were both involved in 26's first creative project: *26 Letters: Illuminating the Alphabet*. He was "Q" and I was "V".

I thought *26 Letters* was a brilliant project. It harnessed the complementary powers of words and design in a fresh and – in terms of the commercial world in which most of us worked – unfettered way. This was the start of something. The flexibility and efficacy of a number, combining the creativity of writers and designers … where next? I wanted to initiate a project that would attract the Scottish creative community to come on board. I also wanted to devise a project so that it had a more commercial angle – to involve business, industry. In Scotland, what better industry than the Scotch Whisky industry. But who would have 26 whiskies for 52 creatives to respond to? Well, it had to be The Scotch Malt Whisky

Society. Luckily I had done some writing for the Society which had gone down well. And they had a brave, passionate, cultured Marketing Manager: Charlotte Halliday.

On 26 August 2004 I floated an idea past Jamie Jauncey and John Simmons.

Team 26 writers with 26 designers. Eighteen teams from Scotland and eight from south of the border. Each team will be invited to a general malt whisky tasting led by one of The Scotch Malt Whisky Society panel where the tasting and nosing process will be gone through and the language of tasting notes explained and discussed. (Also, at this event, a year's free membership to The Scotch Malt Whisky Society for each participant will be activated.) Each team will be given a malt whisky sample, selected by the Society's tasting panel. A creative brief will be issued, devised by the project co-ordinators (there will be design and language guidelines but these will be sensible rather than restrictive: we are looking for original, fresh work). It will then be over to the creative teams to come up with a distinctive, original label for their designated malt.

The original artworks and a display of all labels on bottles will form the basis of an exhibition at 28 Queen Street at the time of the Edinburgh Festival and then transfer to the Society's London venue to coincide with and hopefully be part of the London Design Festival. The actual (filled) bottles of the 26 Malts will be released in batches over the next year, ensuring continued profile for the project. (Each participant will receive a complimentary bottle of their malt). We will approach a publisher to publish a book that will feature the artworks and a diary from each team on the creative process.

This is pretty much what has happened. In October, Charlotte took the idea and floated it past her masters. It engaged their imaginations. By 17 November 2004, in the old Mission Hall that now houses the Scottish Book Trust, Jamie and I announced to a gathering of 12 or so Scottish 26ers that the project was a goer. Old time friend, colleague and designer extraordinaire Damian Mullan came on board. (We'll need him, I thought. In fact we couldn't have done without him.) On 25 January, Burns Night to those that don't know, not a haggis or piper in sight at the London College of Communications where I was embarking on yet another 26 project(!), I bearded Lynne Dobney, Director of the London Design Festival and asked her if 26 Malts could be part of this year's festival. She said yes. Just like that. What a star! Invitations to the 26 membership and the Scottish design community went out on 27 January.

The same day John Simmons wrote to me: *Hi Stuart, Good God, you unleashed something there. Barely an hour after the project invitation went around I already have four writers on the reserve list.* That list bumped up to 26. It's a number that keeps cropping up these days. We had the same response in Scotland.

The rest is charted in these journals. I can only reiterate what I wrote in the exhibition programme notes. The creative output has been amazing; an extraordinarily vibrant and varied response: poems, fibs, teasers, salutations, invitations, *trompe l'oeils*, talking whiskies, responses inspired by tarot and alchemy, bananas and liquorice, rubber tyres and the sweetest of golden honeys. Twenty-six labels liberated from usual brand constraints – an explosion of colour, wit and passion. All testifying to the provocative complexity and allure of Scotch Malt Whisky and the rich diversity achieved through creative collaboration.

So, thank you to everyone who has participated. You've done good. And if nothing else, demonstrated the contribution the imagination can make to a great product. Special thanks to Annabel Meikle who lead groups through a series of inspired tastings and from whom I learnt the more or less oily wonders of "tears", "legs" or "church windows". Special thanks also to Barclay Price of Arts & Business Scotland who stepped in with additional funding to turn the exhibition from "nice to have" into a reality. And other little pieces of my heart to fellow project managers Charlotte Halliday, Damian Mullan and Jamie Jauncey. You made it happen. As I've been prone to say to you all of late: "Your reward's in heaven." I trust it will be more than the statutory angel's share.

JJ: Stuart first floated the malt whisky idea to me shortly after we'd launched 26 in Scotland on a sunny August day at the Edinburgh International Book Festival.

We had both recently taken part in the first big 26 creative project, *26 Letters: Illuminating the Alphabet*, but while the idea of pairing a writer with a designer to interpret a letter of the alphabet had seemed fairly straightforward, applying the same formula to malt whisky seemed to me, well … less obvious.

The more I thought about Stuart's idea, however, the more I realised how inspired it was. Whisky is as much a Scottish icon as tartan and it travels the world as widely. The notion of whisky is deeply embedded in Scottish culture, from the poetry of Burns to the terraces at Hampden Park, the music of Niel Gow to the novels of Ian Rankin. The "craitur" has lubricated untold creative impulses down the centuries, not to mention the appreciation of their fruits.

Within the whisky industry a very particular design idiom has developed over the last forty years, a very particular language too, both strongly suggestive of craft and tradition, natural ingredients, landscape and a sense of the aesthetic. But, with a few notable exceptions, both have become entrenched and so, it seemed to us, ripe for subversion by an irreverent posse of fifty-two writers and designers with creative *cartes blanches*.

By the time of our first meeting with Charlotte Halliday at The Scotch Malt Whisky Society, I felt full of excitement about the whole idea; not least because here was an organisation that could give the creative concept a commercial focus in the form of its 25,000 members, all of whom, we hoped, would want to buy the 26 exotically labelled whiskies we were proposing to serve up.

It was a bold step for the Society, entrusting the good name and reputation of its fine malts to our band of as-yet-unidentified mavericks; but to our delight Charlotte instantly understood our ideas and embraced them with equal enthusiasm. With the addition of Stuart's designer friend, the eternally cheerful and unflappable Damian Mullan, the three-man-and-a-woman project management team was complete.

Had we known then what a massive undertaking it would be, we might never have started. There were so many more strands to the project than we could ever have imagined, and over the winter it seemed that more were coming to the surface each week.

By mid-February we'd identified the candidate whiskies, appointed the creative teams, scheduled the introductory tasting sessions, been turned down by one publisher and almost found another, started planning the exhibitions — one in Edinburgh, one in London, talked with publicists and cajoled other partners (the London Design Festival and Arts & Business) into the project. But despite all this endeavour, it still seemed somehow tentative, a little unreal even.

Then, in March, we held the introductory tasting sessions — two in Edinburgh, one in London — and suddenly, as if we'd uncorked a particularly fine bottle of malt, the whole thing burst alive. The Society opened its doors and Annabel Meikle put us charmingly and expertly through our paces. The fifty-two names, many of them strangers to each other, acquired faces and voices. The cask-strength whisky stung our palates. And we were initiated into the arcane, fragrant and sometimes hilarious language of whisky tasting.

There was a buzz as people left these sessions, making plans to get together once their assigned whiskies materialised. The huge possibilities of the whole thing were beginning to open up in our minds. With this came a buoying sense of collective creative energy; counterpointed, as many of the journals reveal, by a very real sense of apprehension about the unknown experience yet to come.

Over the next three months, as the management of the project became increasingly frantic and demanding, we felt our skins prickle constantly with a kind of static from the swarm of creative ideas that was gathering somewhere just beyond our conscious range.

Finally, at the beginning of June the creative concepts began to arrive. Unpaid for our labours, Stuart, Charlotte, Damian and I had joked that our reward would be in heaven. But this *was* heaven: a banquet of creativity, the laden boards groaning with ideas, themes and styles of execution.

Now, as I write, we're nearly at the finishing post, the artwork for the labels and much of the content of the book ready to go, only the exhibition remaining to be organised. And I find myself struck more than anything by what an extraordinary amount of goodwill this project has generated between people who have never met before.

"This has been a very cool experience," said Nina Gronblom, one of the designers, in her covering email. That gladdens me greatly because it's what we wanted people to feel. It also, I believe, says something very important about the creative process: the more you allow people the freedom to do what comes readily and naturally to them, the more wholeheartedly they will invest in collaboration with other like-minded souls, and the more satisfying the results.

This was certainly my experience of managing the project. Charlotte, Stuart, Damian and I seemed almost effortlessly to divide up the tasks without ever once sitting down to decide who did what. "Four project managers!" a friend snorted. I could see the camel taking shape in his mind, Bactrian at that.

Not so. This project has been a thoroughbred to the core, bursting with spirit in every sense of the word – the spirit of creativity, of collaboration, of co-operation and, of course, the multi-hued, multi-flavoured, multi-aroma'd, multifaceted spirit that has inspired the labels in the pages that follow.

CREOSOTE TO COCONUT

CHARLES MACLEAN ON THE LANGUAGE OF WHISKY

"Smells detonate softly in our memory like poignant landmines hidden under the weedy mass of the years. Hit a tripwire of smell and memories explode at once. A complex vision leaps out of the undergrowth."

Diane Ackerman, *A Natural History of the Senses*

Central to the 26 Malts project is the character of the whiskies we were asked to examine, their flavour, style and personality. But how do you define character? What words can you use to describe flavour? In this essay I will look at how "the language of whisky" has evolved, so you can see how the contributors to the book have defied convention!

Flavour

"Flavour" has three aspects – aroma, texture and taste – and of these, aroma is the most important. See how little you can "taste" when you hold your nose. Yet until the late 1980s no attempt was made by whisky companies to communicate the virtues of their brands in terms of their aromatic characteristics.

Scotch was for drinking. Texture and taste were sometimes addressed – both invariably described as "smooth", "rounded" or "mature" – although some brands stressed "taste the difference", without saying what the difference might be. But never aroma. Real men smell their wine, but they don't smell their whisky. Leave this to the back-room boys in blending houses.

Recently, I was given some albums of whisky ads from the 1970s and 1980s. Strange what people collect, but a useful reminder. The focus of brand advertising is reflected by the strap-lines:

Heritage (e.g. "Born 1820, still going strong" – Johnnie Walker. The line was invented in 1909).

Consistency (e.g. "Quality in an age of change" – The Famous Grouse. The slogan served Grouse well for two decades from 1972).

Scottish-ness (e.g. "Scotland's Prince of Whiskies" – Chivas Regal. Invented by Bill Bernbach, after DDB won the account in 1962).

Lifestyle (e.g. "The good life. Ballantine's is part of it". Updated with contemporary style shots, but still rooted in pre-war huntin', shootin' and fishin' imagery).

Authenticity (e.g. "Handcrafted by the Sixteen Men of Tain" – Glenmorangie. This memorable campaign accompanied Glenmorangie's launch as a single malt in 1981).

Aspects of production (e.g. "Double matured" – both Whyte & Mackay and Cutty Sark. The reference is to transferring the blend to marrying casks prior to bottling, the standard industry practice at this time).

It took the growth in interest in single malts in the 1980s – the growth in whisky connoisseurship – to make it reasonable to describe and even promote whisky in terms of its aroma and flavour.

Pioneering tasting notes

A pioneer in the field of supplying tasting notes was The Scotch Malt Whisky Society, founded by a group of friends in 1983. In the early days the language they used tended to be cautious, however. The three "Island" whiskies listed in my earliest *Newsletter* (No. 17, August 1987) are described as having "a peaty, malty, vanilla aroma typical of this whisky", "a slightly peaty, vanilla aroma" and a "distinctive peaty, smoky aroma".

The same year as these notes were written, Wallace Milroy published his *Malt Whisky Almanac*, the first book to supply tasting notes for Scotch. As with the Society, his notes are reserved: the three whiskies mentioned above are described merely as "lovely peaty aroma, with a hint of sweetness", "fine and fruity" and "light, fresh with a trace of peat".

Simple notes compared with what we would expect today, but a step in the right direction. Remember, these were the days before Oz Clarke and Jilly Goolden de-mystified the language of wine tasting: the "classic" language of wine tasting was (and is) tight-lipped and coded. I quote a random example of the style from my 1998 *Guide to Burgundy en Primeur* which describes that year's Cote de Nuits as: "… well structured, rich and highly concentrated aromas. Tannins are firm, fine and balanced by weight of fruit and rich textures."

Such coded language was never a problem for whisky tasting notes, since there was (and is) no prescribed language, no "correct" way of describing flavour.

Flavour terminology in Scotch whisky

Although no attempt was made to describe flavour to consumers before about 1988, aromatic descriptors had long been used by distillers and blenders. But each company had – and still has, to some extent – its own vocabulary.

Much work was done in the 1970s by the Distillers Company Limited, under the direction of Dr Magnus Pike, better known as the first TV "crazy scientist". In these days the DCL was deeply secretive about everything, so this work was not shared with the so-called "independent" whisky companies (i.e. non-DCL).

Inter alia, Pike and his colleagues evolved a vocabulary to describe new-make spirit character. Early versions were based on chemical abbreviations and even numbers – 1 = feinty, 2 = estery, etc., made possible by the fact that the team doing sensory evaluation all knew exactly what the numbers represented. Later this evolved into the categories used currently by DCL's successor, Diageo plc:

NEW MAKE SPIRIT

Character	Descriptors	Character	Descriptors
Clean	No specific character	Perfumed	Scented, fragrant, floral
Fruity	Fruit, fruit gums, pear drops, bubble gum	Sour	Sickly, butyric acid ("baby vomit")
Green/grassy	Apples, hay, cut grass	Spicy	Cake mix, soapy, bread-like, baking
Green/oily	Linseed, putty		
Meaty	Marmite, burnt, boiled cabbage	Sulphury	Drains, eggy, spent matches, DMTS
Metallic	Metallic		
Musty	Old books, bung cloths, damp	Sweet	Butterscotch, toffee, caramel, buttery
Nutty	Iron tonic, bran, pot ale, mousy		
Peaty	Peat reek, phenolic, smoky, carbolic	Vegetable	Pea pods, onions, turnips, DMS
		Waxy	Candle wax, beeswax

The independent companies charged Pentlands Scotch Whisky Research in Edinburgh with the task of developing a common flavour terminology which would "enable the product to be discussed with greater precision and clarity, acceptable and understood across the industry". Pentlands' working party comprised George Shortreed (blender with J&B), Paul Rickards (blender with Robertson & Baxter), Jim Swan and Sheila Burtles (both sensory chemists on Pentlands' staff). They reported in 1979.

During the course of the study they consulted "26 persons [sic!] involved in distilling, blending and R&D", and adopted a wheel design to present their findings. Such a device was not new – the brewing industry had previously used a wheel for displaying odour groups – but it was, literally, revolutionary within the whisky industry.

In 2000 the "Pentlands Wheel" was revised and simplified by scientists from the Department of Bioscience at the University of Strathclyde and the Scotch Whisky Research Institute.

The Revised Flavour Wheel has a "hub" or "primary tier" divided into 12 "principal aromatic groups" – Peaty, Grainy, Fruity, Floral, Feints, Woody, Sweet, Stale, Sulphury, Cheesy and Oily – a segment for "Primary taste", and one for "Mouth and Nasal effect".

The second tier sub-divided these segments into 50 "secondary groups" and beyond this were third tier terms further refining the odours which might be encountered.

For example, the first three segments read:

Primary term	Second tier	Third tier
Peaty	Medicinal	TCP, antiseptic, Germoline, hospitals
	Smoky	Wood smoke, kippery, smoked bacon/cheese
	Burnt	Tar, soot, ash
Grainy	Cereal	Digestive biscuits, husky, bran, leathery, tobacco, mousy
	Malt	Malt extract, malted barley
	Mash	Porridge, draff, wort, cooked maize
Fruity	Solventy	Nail varnish remover, paint thinner, fusel oil
	Orchard	Apple, peaches, pear
	Tropical	Pear-drop, banana, pineapple, melon
	Citrus	Orange, lemon, grapefruit, zest
	Berries	Tomato stem, blackcurrant, catty
	Dried	Raisins, figs, prunes

This is a very useful guide, but it was devised for the industry and embraces new make character as well as that of mature whisky, so can be confusing to the lay consumer. Also, it is important to remember that the descriptive terms are for guidance only. The suggested vocabulary, even the divisions of "primary odours", are not set in stone; indeed, other eight- or six- or even four-tier wheels are commonly used. The language is open to individual interpretation and expansion, or contraction.

Analytical nosing

Sensory chemists talk of two kinds of "tasting" – the correct term is "organoleptic assessment": analytical (or objective) and hedonic (or subjective – the word derives from "hedonism", the pursuit of pleasure).

From a linguistic perspective, the analytical panel, whose job it is to be as objective as possible – to describe "only what is there" – will have a tightly controlled vocabulary, not unlike the words listed above to describe new-make character. The words themselves do not matter: the key factor is that all members of the panel know exactly what they mean when they describe an odour as "leathery" or "nutty-spicy" or "green", etc.

Chemists have wrestled for years with the challenge of identifying fundamental "primary" odours, from which all others spring, notably John E. Amoore in Berkeley in the late 1970s, who concluded that "the total number of human primary odors is at least 32". If you bear in mind that there are only four primary tastes – sweet, sour, salty and bitter (some include a fifth, "umami" – the taste of monosodium glutamate), out of which all other tastes are constructed; if you consider that our visual universe is built from only three primary colours – you will appreciate the vastness of the Kingdom of Smell …

Hedonic nosing

By contrast, the hedonic panel encourages its members to give free reign to subjective interpretation, no matter how personal or potentially ludicrous. This is where the fun starts.

Of course, subjective analysis is based upon an objective source – the odour-bearing, volatile molecules which trigger responses in our olfactory system. There are two stages to a "nosing", as it is termed in the whisky trade: isolating an aroma from a complex of aromas, and describing it. The interpretation and articulation of these responses are entirely personal, based upon individual experience.

Smell is our most primitive sense, and unlike our other senses, it is not mediated: it is plugged directly into the limbic system of the cortex, which is also the seat of our emotions and of our memories. No wonder smells are so powerfully evocative!

When we smell something, we draw, consciously or subconsciously, upon our memory bank, not only in relation to "having smelled that smell before", but also in terms of what it reminds us of, and – here is the primitive bit – whether we automatically like or dislike it.

Like well-hung game, Gorgonzola cheese or Bombay duck, whisky is an acquired taste. It is unlikely to appeal to younger people, unless its taste is disguised – notwithstanding the efforts of the whisky industry to recruit this market. A bad experience with whisky out of teenage bravado can take years to overcome. I scunnered myself (to use the Scots term) for smoky Islay whisky for two years, after an especially dramatic night in Port Ellen in 1971 ...

Memory and imagery

Rising above positive aversion – "Don' like that" – let us return to how we describe the aroma of whisky.

Commonly, we use figurative language – similes and metaphors –likening one sensation to another, or describing a smell in terms of what it resembles. Thus, we might justifiably say "wet dog", "sheep dip" or "creosote" to describe a pungent Islay whisky; "nail varnish remover", "green apples", "ice cream" or "coconut" to describe a Speyside, matured in American oak. It will be noted that "reminds me of ..." is implicit in all these descriptors.

We might go further in our imagery: "it reminds me of my uncle's car", "Christmas at my grandparents", "blowing bubble-gum in the bicycle sheds at school" (childhood memories, particularly of confectionery, are very common!). Cynics say this is too personal to communicate anything. On the contrary. Such similes are "portmanteau terms" and, with only a little imagination, carry a raft of meaning. Depending upon the age of the speaker, the "uncle's car" is maybe a vintage car, with all those smells of leather, rubber, oil and exhaust fumes that made me feel car-sick as a child. "Christmas" is baking, cooking smells, candlewax, open fires, pine needles. "Bubble-gum" is a descriptor for estery notes, found in all whiskies.

Abstract terms – popular with oenophiles – are also useful, although open to misinterpretation. Look at the list below. When you say it smells "young" do you mean "lithe" and "vigorous" or "immature"? When you say "mellow", do you mean "well-rounded" or "boring"? Abstract terms also give rise to what linguists call "contrasting pairs", and together these can be useful as a general guide to the character of the whisky. For example:

Smooth	Rough	Coarse	Refined	Mellow	Hard
Clean	Dirty	Light	Heavy	Young	Old
Fresh	Stale	Rich	Thin	etc.	etc.

In conclusion

I say again, the words we use to describe the aromas found in whisky are not defined, not set in stone. There are no rights and wrongs – although if you smell "sweaty socks" and everyone else on the panel smells "roses", you may have a condition called "specific anosmia" or "odour blindness".

Use your imagination. Dredge your own memory. Be brave. Concentrate. It is not easy to put words to smells, but it enhances your enjoyment, and is great fun! Lots of practice is essential, many samples of fine malt whisky are required!

"Smell is our most seductive and provocative sense, invading every domain of our lives, providing the single most powerful link to our distant origins ... But it is also mute, almost unspeakable, defying description and collection, challenging the imagination."

Lyall Watson, *Jacobson's Organ*

A SNAPSHOT FROM THE MEMORY BOX

ANNABEL MEIKLE OF THE SCOTCH MALT WHISKY SOCIETY ON THE SENSE OF SMELL

For a couple of years between being a potter and my current job as a whisky taster for The Scotch Malt Whisky Society, I was a cheese buyer for Edinburgh's world famous delicatessen, Valvona and Crolla. As a child I had frequented the place with my mother who had a special shopping list reserved for this special shop. I remember the counter seemed high and intimidating and was framed by a daunting array of bulbous cheeses, fiery dried chillies and knobbly salamis which hung from butcher's hooks. The counter itself was filled with bowls of small glossy olives and legs of prosciutto; indeed every surface spilled over with strange and inviting foods I had never seen before …. And then there was the smell!

I had forgotten this experience until I walked into the shop many years later to ask for a job. The second I stepped back inside the aromas bombarded me – ground coffee, rich cheeses, cured meats, chocolate, ripe peaches – all mixed together in one intoxicating blast. Instantly, the sights, sounds and smells of the shopping trips with my mother came flooding back. This is what our sense of smell can do. It can trigger a snapshot from our memory box, an instant recollection from one simple aroma.

So what does the sense of smell mean to me? During my years as a potter I relied on vision and touch, never valuing my sense of smell. Fair enough, I thought, after all how relevant is smell to daily life?

Well, more than you would imagine and that's the beauty of it. As our sense of smell operates on a subliminal level, we don't even realise it's at work. We encounter thousands of aromas a day, filtering them and sending messages to our brain. Luckily our brain prioritises this information and helps us define what we need to react to, otherwise our sensory system would overload with too much information.

Examples of this "higher-order processing" include: is what are we about to put in our mouth good or rotten? We smell decay and immediately are repulsed by the food and so protect ourselves from eating something that will make us ill. Or we smell good cooking smells and our mouths water and we are reminded to eat.

Higher-order processing is essential as it helps to keep us alive. So much so that the part of our brain that deals with smell was one of the first to develop in the evolutionary process. It is closely linked to our emotional state which is why smell can influence our mood.

When it comes to nosing whisky, the first impression is very important as this instant reaction can be pleasurable – or not. To illustrate this, I usually finish a tutored tasting with a heavily peated whisky. The response is instant and always vocal. Such phenolic whiskies trigger responses that remind us of antiseptic, swimming pools, carbolic soap, creosoted fences or smoky fires.

The association that these smells hold for you determines your emotional attachment to this whisky. Personally, I adore a peaty dram because it reminds me of the smell of my father when he came home from work. As a consultant surgeon and a gentleman, he insisted on doing his ward round in a tweed jacket. The smells of the hospital clung to the fabric. When he came home he would pour himself a dram and I would perch on his knee. As a result, the smell of hospitals and whisky are mingled in my mind.

At the beginning of a whisky tasting, I explain that drinking whisky is an overall sensory experience, a blending of sensations. Fortunately all the equipment we need for this experience is in the portable kit which is conveniently contained in our heads! In other words, the nose, mouth, tongue and brain. Our taste buds, the olfactory epithelium and retinal cells process the information that emerges from the glass. They are converted into electrical signals and passed to the brain. The orbitofrontal cortex cleverly knits together the information of aroma and taste, producing what we recognise as flavour. It draws our response to the mouthfeel and colour of the whisky and marries all this information in our mouth. Armed with all this sensory feedback, we can access our response to the whisky – and if it is a fine example we experience hedonistic valence, or pleasure to you and me.

At the tasting we unravel the knitting as we dissect the different elements in the glass. We observe the colour often describing it in metallic terms, copper, antique gold or silvery. If I have a female group I suggest hair colours, blonde, auburn, henna as these descriptors help engage their imaginations.

Then the nose – what's the first thing that hits you? We have a limited language for smell and use words generally associated with taste. However if you liken the smells to those of everyday life, the scope is endless – foods, flowers, sweeties, farmyards and hospitals. By associating the smell with an experience it creates a picture, such as apple pies baking in granny's kitchen.

At the Society our whiskies are carefully selected by an independent tasting panel. As each cask of whisky has unique qualities, the panel creates an individual tasting note to illustrate what you might find in the glass. Sometimes our descriptors have a confessional aspect to them, "licking a nine volt battery" or "orange oil rubbed on a wet suit!" As you can see, there is no wrong or right answer – it is a personal reaction. Discussion is always encouraged at this point, and I often hear the comment, "I just can't put my finger on what it is". Then someone will suggest parma violets which elicits the response, "Yes – that's exactly it!"

And then to the taste and finish. The texture of the dram can be hot, burning, prickly or cool, smooth and silky. Some drams can make your teeth "itch" or your tongue curl. Others have a lingering finish that you can still taste on the way home. The taste can be as sweet as vanilla sugar or caramel, toffee or honey. These are the trademarks of a spirit matured in a cask that previously held Bourbon. It can emerge as desiccated coconut or ground almonds. Or it can be dry and tannic, heady and musky with Christmas cake and dark fruits hinting at a sherry influence.

Attending the Society's tasting panel pushes you to be more precise. I remember an early experience with the experts. Dipping my nose into the glass I mumbled something about smoke, whereupon Charlie MacLean, the Chair of the Panel pounced on me. "What kind of smoke? Is it a freshly lit pipe or stale cigar smoke, leaves burning on a bonfire or peat on a bothy fire? Heather burning or charcoal on the beach? Struck match or blown out candle? What?" I soon learnt to be a little more specific. I also recollect Charlie pinpointing an aroma as pink almonds; not white or yellow ones but *pink!*

So many whiskies and so many experiences to be had.

WHAT'S IN A LABEL?

STUART DELVES AND DAMIAN MULLAN

A label is one of the oldest and most powerful tools of branding. It is a stamp of guaranteed quality and consistency. It is a stamp of authorship and ownership and should be worn with pride. Branding, as we know it, really began in the late nineteenth century and the matter of quality and consistency was very much at the heart of whisky distilling as it still is today.

Before 1845 glass was taxed, and clear glass was taxed some eleven times the rate of dark glass. This meant bottles were precious and those who were grand enough and could afford it often embellished their bottles with their coats of arms. Bottles would be taken to the wine merchants to be filled. Those who couldn't afford bottles would take earthenware jugs. And often, at the lower end of the market scurrilous retailers were known to adulterate their wares – in the case of whisky, with shellac, tartaric, acetic acids, acetic ether, oil of wine, spirit of nitrous ether, glycerine and green tea!

When the tax on glass was lifted manufacturers, concerned to establish and maintain a name for their products, started bottling spirits and wines. This effectively gave them quality control. Thus the label was born, a stamp of authority, saying who had made the stuff in the bottle. And from there all sorts of other descriptions would follow in terms of verifying content and volume and country of origin. Whisky was at the forefront of this drive for authenticity and on the following two pages we have displayed a range of early whiskies: simple, unpretentious and some of them strangely modern in their minimalism.

And we should thank the label really, for it guards against unscrupulousness and that ghastly list above.

Branding of course has become a very sophisticated matter. On the facing page are examples of two of today's leading Scotch Malt Whisky brands. See how they contrast with the labels overleaf and then with the Society's current label (below).

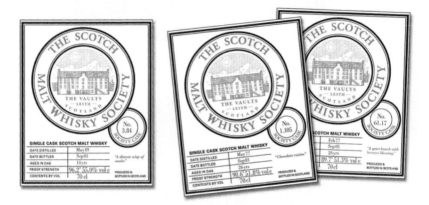

This is The Scotch Malt Whisky's current stock label. It hasn't changed much since the Society was founded in the 1970s. It's unaffected and much loved. Members say that its minimal design (more akin to a "house" style) ensures that nothing detracts from the quality of what's inside. There's an appreciation of the modesty of the numbering system and the cask number. It's even said that when a Society bottle sits alongside other malts in the cabinet at home it doesn't compete because it doesn't have to. The contents are a given: they will be superb. And yet, here's the paradox, each bottling is unique and unrepeatable. That's what 26 Malts has celebrated with such diverse words and imagery. What will the members say? The Society are expecting letters. Oh yes. Some from "Disgusted of Tunbridge Wells" and some from "Delighted of Auchendinny". Which "D" will you rally round?

THANKS TO CHARLES MACLEAN FOR SOURCE MATERIAL.

26

CASK NUMBER

64.8

John Allert John has worked in branding for the past sixteen years, firstly as a designer, then as a strategist, and more recently as CEO of Interbrand Australia. In late 2003 he was appointed chief operating officer of Interbrand UK, and to the global board of Interbrand Corporation. A regular media commentator, he is currently writing his first book. **Patrick Bergel** Patrick is a freelance writer, designer and art director, although not necessarily in that order. His clients include Unilever, Orange and Virgin. In 2001, he founded a company to build social networking software. He currently develops search engines for mobile devices and works on earthbound branding projects.

PATRICK'S JOURNAL

John Allert and I managed to avoid each other at the first tasting, but we introduced ourselves a week later on a hot day in a dark theatre bar off the Strand.

Almost at once was the eerie sensation that John and I had met before, had talked before, had done all of this before. It was as if we knew exactly what had happened, and what surely must happen again.

Neither of us spoke openly about it. There was no need.

We decided that our label would be the best. To that end, John at once shyly offered the idea that we would adopt for this project: the dialogue between taste and taster, or as he put it, "an argument on your tongue, a lovers' quarrel," the critical moment that commanded attention, demanded resolution.

Some time later we were sent a bottle that had cracked in transit. We had no choice but to sample the precious liquid from John's sodden memoranda, sucking at the fine Italian leather of his splendid briefcase. We laughed like schoolgirls as we picked broken glass from our tongues, drunken, carefree.

SACRED LOVE TAKES AIM AT THE SOUL

Sit In Amore Reciproca

Les traits d'Amour ne sont mortel
Lors qu'ils se rendent mutuels .

Mich. van Lochom . exeud .

Plustost que d'estre prisonniere
D'Amante ie seray guerriere .

SACRED LOVE TEACHES THE SOUL TO FIGHT

Qui docet manus meas
ad prœlium . Pf. 17.

Mich. van Lochom exeud .

Then we paused to soberly consider how best we might unify our chosen theme and our tasting notes in visual form.

The challenge accepted, we lay around almost motionless for days under the cool glass tables at Interbrand. We yawned, stretched, slept, sang old Phoenician sea-shanties, and played endless games of chance with chicken bones as improvised dice. We scratched at ourselves incessantly and for many weeks lived mostly off rotting fruit. At that time we were too lazy to climb for the fresh yellow pears that were left for us by terrified assistants. We sneered at passers-by. We disrupted meetings. We grew ugly.

On the thirty-third morning in the boardroom, I found a startling woodcut of a looming black mountain in my bedclothes. Although it was clearly signed "Margaret" there could be no doubt it was in my own hand. Evidently, I had made the work while in some kind of horrid trance-state, undoubtedly induced by having eaten the blue flowers that grew in abundance behind the photocopier. We had by then made a solemn compact, a blood-oath that our art would feature "neither crags nor stags," and so John cursed me for a fool, threatening to beat me to death with the arm of his chair if I showed it to anyone. Ashamed, I shredded the image again and again.

At sunrise on day eighty, a replacement bottle arrived, this time intact, brought by a messenger-boy with plastic wings on his shoes. We drank again, this time not as apes or artists, but as scientists.

Thanks in no small part to our informal network of child spies, we tracked down an engineer from Imperial Soap with access to a McKinley-Sciex mass spectrometer. The engineer (a moral weakling, additionally burdened with heavy gambling debts) was squarely confronted with public exposure and left to consider the outcome. We were kindly granted full use of the Spectral Analysis Facility by night. Gas chromatography soon told us what our taste buds could not: the precise chemical composition of our malt. Wide-eyed, we saw inside the liquid: vertiginous spikes of cold ether plunging into sugared valleys, precipices of carbon and caramel. The data was conclusive, final, irrefutable and yet ... lacked mystery. We threw it to one side. We burnt the graphs and paid off the engineer.

That night, disappointed but unbowed, we returned to our original theme, as if coming home. We returned to whisky as story, as wordless argument, a liquid philosophy, resolution as pleasure.

And we found what we believed was our solution in an old handbook for an abandoned magical science: the science of alchemy.

We hope you like it.

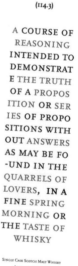

(114.3)

A COURSE OF
REASONING
INTENDED TO
DEMONSTRAT
E THE TRUTH
OF A PROPOS
ITION OR SER
IES OF PROPO
SITIONS WITH
OUT ANSWERS
AS MAY BE FO
-UND IN THE
QUARRELS OF
LOVERS, IN A
FINE SPRING
MORNING OR
THE TASTE OF
WHISKY

Single Cask Scotch Malt Whisky
Aged in oak (12yrs)
Contents by vol (50cl)
Vol (54.5%) e
Bottled by The Scotch Malt Whisky Society

64.8

26

MALTS

CASK NUMBER

29.44

Nick Asbury Nick was a director of creative consultancy Other before turning freelance. He now writes extensively for and about the design business. He is the co-author of the forthcoming *Alas! Smith & Milton: How not to run a design company.* Craig Barnes Craig was a record company marketing manager for ten years, until he grew weary of both the music and the business. He is studying at Chelsea School of Art & Design and thoroughly enjoying going back to the start again.

NICK'S DIARY

Having written just the four words for the label itself, it seems a fair division of labour for me to have a go at the diary. It's based on a loose amalgam of Craig's recollections and mine and includes liberal amounts of post-rationalisation, designed to make us appear cleverer and more in control of events than we were at the time.

We conducted the tasting late one Friday afternoon at Chelsea College of Art. Finding a spare workroom with a reasonably sturdy table, we poured ourselves a modest measure and noted with some trepidation that this already represented about two thirds of the bottle's contents. There wouldn't be many chances to taste this stuff, so we'd better make the most of it. What followed was a tense round of swirling, sniffing, sipping and chin-stroking. We bandied around words like citrusy, salty, peaty and fiery. Craig even weighed in with an impressive "astringent". But the truest reactions were probably our first, mine consisting of a well-thought-out "Cor" while Craig found himself suppressing the urge to giggle.

We subsequently managed to agree on three things. First of all, this was clearly a very strong whisky. We knew a lot of these single-cask malts were strong, but this felt unusually powerful. Secondly, there was a distinct fieriness to it; not just the normal, alcoholic fieriness you'd expect from any whisky, but something that lingered in the flavour and smell itself. Thirdly, it tasted great. After a few more

THE WHOLE WORLD'S A BOOZE

AND LIFE IS BUT A DRAM

WHEN THE BOTTLE GETS EMPTY

IT SURE AIN'T WORTH A DAMN

WORTHWHILE TALK FOR BOOZE & DRUGS, 1970
CASK NO (114.3.) SINGLE CASK SCOTCH MALT WHISKY
AGED IN OAK (12YRS) CONTENTS BY VOL (50CL)
VOL (54.5%) E
BOTTLED BY THE SCOTCH MALT WHISKY SOCIETY

thank you and goodnight

CASK NO (114.3.) CONTENTS BY VOL (50CL)
AGED IN OAK (12YRS) VOL (54.5%) E
SINGLE CASK SCOTCH MALT WHISKY
BOTTLED BY THE SCOTCH MALT WHISKY SOCIETY

sips, we agreed we were not only working on the most brilliant job ever but were also best mates.

Craig soon started talking about the way visitors to art galleries can spend more time looking at the descriptive cards next to the paintings than at the paintings themselves. He wondered whether the same thing applied here: you can get so hung up on reading the label and tasting notes that you forget to enjoy the taste. We thought we could nod towards this by creating a label in the style of a gallery card, perhaps adding a red sticker to each bottle as it was sold. It entertained us for a while, perhaps because of our arty surroundings, but it all seemed a bit too tricksy. There was no need to elevate whisky into a work of art in order to appreciate it.

Meanwhile, I found myself thinking about King Kong, particularly the part when he is captured and shipped off to civilisation. Whatever we were drinking, it probably originated on some windswept outcrop somewhere and here we were in a Chelsea art studio drinking it out of a couple of IKEA glasses and diluting it with Evian. It felt like there was an idea in this: a mysterious force of nature bottled and tamed, but refusing to take its fate lying down. Maybe it would lead somewhere, maybe not. The main thing we kept returning to was this idea of burning. We adjourned for a pint, thought about it some more and then went our separate ways, both feeling very sleepy.

Craig subsequently went to South Africa for a couple of weeks and, on the flight back, witnessed a particularly spectacular sunset. He made a note of the way the sun sinking into the ocean separated out into rich, complex bands of colour. On his return, he dropped me an email and we agreed there was a nice parallel in this. During the tasting, Craig had been intrigued by how the whisky also separated out and revealed its complexity as it came into contact with water. While sunsets seemed a bit of a cliché for a whisky label, we thought a more abstract treatment might be interesting. Craig began experimenting to see what effects he could produce out of a four-colour process.

For some reason, we also found ourselves thinking about song lyrics. Craig had Johnny Cash's *Ring of Fire* in his head. I had a Bob Dylan version of a folk song called *Moonshiner*. I mentioned the lyrics of the last verse to Craig: "The whole world's a bottle / And life is but a dram / When the bottle gets empty / It sure ain't worth a damn." Craig pointed out that the lyrics could be read as an irreverent comment on the project itself, something I hadn't spotted. Further research revealed the song is also known as *The Bottle Song*, which somehow added to its appeal. We used the lines on one of our two initial routes, set against an image Craig had been toying with ever since the first meeting: an explosion of colour reminiscent of a firework. There was something about the idea of fireworks that felt right: the pent-up energy, the burning fuse, the sudden explosion and lingering trails of colour. As a combination of words and imagery, we didn't think it tied together yet, but it was a start.

The other route was a development of Craig's abstract sunset, with layers of overlapping colours producing a dreamy, soporific effect. I'd been pondering this for a while and scribbled down the line "Thank you and goodnight". It seemed to reflect the sunset idea and the intense character of the whisky, suggesting both a moment of triumph and an imminent descent into slumber.

The feedback was split fifty-fifty between the two routes and we somehow ended up choosing to do what creatives are meant to hate doing: we took the visual from one route and the line from the other. "Thank you and goodnight" had grown on both of us and we realised that the fireworks image could fit quite nicely, capturing the celebratory feeling of the line. The tone of the execution also felt right: loose, handmade and not too precious. In the end, it was an idea drawn from two casks rather than one, but it seemed to do the trick. We hope the result is worthy of the bottle's contents.

thank you and goodnight

Contents by vol 50cl : Vol 58.4%
de-Fork Scotch Malt Whisky · Cask no.29.44 · Aged in oak 13 years
Produce of Scotland · Bottled by the Scotch Malt Whisky Society

26

CASK NUMBER

2.62

Will Awdry Will is an advertising writer turned creative director at DDB London. In real life, he talks a good book, but has yet to write one. Small children, hopelessness, and meandering encounters with both grape and grain seem to get in the way. Rodney Mylius & Kyn Taylor Rodney and Kyn are part of the new creative studio called Fortune Street. Based on Bankside, a spit from the river Thames, the company specialises in brand identity and design. They are currently working across Europe in Holland, Russia and Turkey. In the UK they continue to creatively direct for the new "Your M&S".

A SPOONFUL OF SUGAR

Initial Consultation, 21 March 2005

The Monday before Easter, I find myself ascending the stairs of The Scotch Malt Whisky Society in London. After a flurry of emails and some extreme patience from the Society's officers, we three and one other have been granted special (late) audience to initiate us into the alchemical mysteries of malt whisky. We are the stragglers on the project. It is a grey, bluff day, rendered Dickensian by street names. Bleeding Heart Yard drips with glorious Victorian menace. By contrast, the signing-in book and stairs to the Society's rooms are neat and prim.

We arrange ourselves under the watchful eye of the delightful Anne Griffiths. Rodney Mylius, one of *the* names in the designer and branding world, has a CV that includes a year in Japan as visiting Professor of Design and more gongs than you can shake a stick at. Lest the reputation seem intimidating, Rodney in person is a Labrador of enthusiasm. Seemingly without effort, he bounds into our opening conversations with a positive, infectious enthusiasm. Kyn, his colleague, whom I am also meeting for the first time, is a quieter study, pursing his lips as he considers the table, decked out with water flasks, tasting glasses and Society paraphernalia.

Anne approaches her subject with warmth and captivating ease. The four of us (our other attendee, John Allert, represents a different group), are unsure as to whether to play attentive schoolboys or hail-fellow-well-met whisky grandees. Anne dispels the role-playing, corrals us into a nicely relaxed place and we hang off her every word. Shyly, we confess our virginity to the language, the ritual and the protocol of whisky tasting.

Trotting through three, very different malts, our reserve is cast aside. We start chucking descriptions at each other with abandon. Some are way off beam, others pin-sharp in nailing the flavours swirling round our glasses.

We journey from Spey to Islands via such phrases as "wet leather" (questionable), "smoked haddock" (bang on, to my nose) and "chewed HB pencil" (jury still deliberating, I believe).

All too soon, our initial consultation is over and we tumble down the stairs to our various other lives for the next week or six …

Diagnosis, 18 May 2005

Freshly off crutches, I limp past the Tate Modern and into the cool vault of Fortune Street's studio space. Rodney and Kyn welcome me, glasses at the ready.

From my bag, I produce the medicine bottle of amber liquid that will affect our thoughts for the next few days of our life. It isn't very big. It has a functional appearance, much like the Tate Modern next door, with a label that declares it is from Distillery 2 and is Sample No. 4. That is all. The serif face and austere information has a whiff of Miss Brodie about it.

I splash the whisky into some glasses and we set to. Straight away, it is abundantly clear we have something special. The three of us shout out flavours as they strike us, oil men lucky enough to hit a rich seam on their first drill; "tea with sugar"; "honey"; "maple syrup"; "rich, buttery, rounded"; "caramel liqueur"; "French … er, cognac". The latter is greeted not as weird but strangely appropriate. "Pudding whisky" is another that sets us nodding.

Ideas pour out in rather more profusion than there are drops in the bottle. We add a little water to help our understanding of its true flavour, and the bottle is soon empty and lifeless. Not so Rodney, who fires ideas into the conversation like a machine gun. Kyn and I rouse ourselves to keep up.

It is clear we have a sweet – or the illusion of sweet – malt on our hands. The cognac notion is the first to bear visual fruit with the idea of a French style whisky. We bat "Gallic goes Gaelic" around, and Kyn and Rodney are inspired to give this face over the next few days.

However, our considered verdict is that this requires too much explanation.

Jackie Wilson's "I Get the Sweetest Feeling" is mentioned. "Sugar Sugar" too, by The Archies. Our age is telling. There is a thought to print the lyrics on the label, but copyright problems put paid to it. Sweeties and the idea of "Bonbon Whisky" tickle our fancy. A few days on, Kyn sets to with a trio of fun thoughts to add substance to this whimsy.

We continue, Rodney still leading the charge, towards notions of Christmas Whisky. From here, it is a short hop to Christening Whisky, an occasion where sweetness prevails. "Head Wetter" emerges as a candidate name before we move on to "Honeymoon Malt". There is also a call to bring the fat, cherubic quality of our sample to life in a seaside postcard way – the Bunter-esque, Skegness-Is-So-Bracing, Toby Jug quality of Thirties and Forties graphic art in mind.

After a couple of hours of musing and scribbling, it is time to go. Like fruit machine wheels, our thoughts rotate round various sugary imaginings for several days, until Kyn sends through a new design thought.

Among the alternatives on this theme, one stands out. A traditional honey spoon drips longs tears of unctuous joy, with a playful rendering of the words "The Sweetest Feeling" typographically stacked to engage the reader who has to decode them. It summarises not only the extraordinary malt we received in the draw, but the experience of messing about, dreaming up the label design too.

We three agree to champion it. Fortunately, so do the team running the project. Kyn and Rodney provide the finishing touches and our baby is off to the races.

All that remains is for us, as an *arriviste* English trio, to implore you to try our particular whisky. It is a truly remarkable drop.

THE
SWEET
FEELI
EST
NG

SINGLE CASK SCOTCH MALT WHISKY
CASK NO. 2.62 - AGED IN OAK 16 YEARS
VOL 57.8% VOL 50CLℯ
PRODUCED IN SCOTLAND
BOTTLED BY THE SCOTCH MALT WHISKY SOCIETY

26

CASK NUMBER

3.109

Alan Black When I started Blackad Copywriting in 1999, I promised never to write one of those self-congratulatory biography paragraphs. So here I am, trying to get to the end of these 40 words without jangling my fulsome credentials at you. Result. Ultan Coyle Unusually likes thinking about Noddy.

TO HELL AND BACK

Ultan and Alan's guide to creating a whisky label

Our introductory tasting in The Vaults went well enough – but the real revelations were formed after we'd mulled and slurped the sample whiskies. (The whisky we'd be working on wasn't due to arrive until the end of April.)

We agreed almost instantly that we wanted to avoid any of the usual whisky clichés; you know, woodcut illustrations, florid language and A Very Particular Way of Setting Type.

No – we would have to go back to the whisky itself.

Another take on taste

After the introductory tasting, I contacted one of my clients with the view to helping out on a tasting experiment.

The client in question was Colin Hopkins from Matthew Algie. They're the UK's leading independent coffee roaster—supplying big names such as Marks & Spencer and Pret A Manger. Colin is their Brand Manager.

One of the things that make Matthew Algie so special (and there are lots of things, trust me) is their investment in sensory analysis.

This branch of science works to understand people's perceptions of food and drink products. In most coffee companies, the game starts and

stops with a professional taster. At Matthew Algie, they do things a little differently. By developing their own easy-to-use coffee vocabulary – and hiring lay people – they run their own tasting panels.

This allows Matthew Algie to find out what real people think about real coffee.

Ultan and I are confirmed whisky novices, so the thought of running a "real" tasting event really appealed.

Whisky-not-so-galore

We received our sample whisky right on time – at the end of April. This was around seven weeks after our introductory tasting, so we were keen to get started.

However, the sample bottle immediately caused us a problem – it was absolutely tiny.

We soon discovered this is normal in the world of professional whisky tasting. However, as we were pinning our creative hopes on a far-from-professional tasting, it was obvious we'd need more whisky.

Charlotte Halliday from The Scotch Malt Whisky Society very kindly pleaded for another sample on our behalf. In the meantime, all we could do was wait and quietly panic as the deadline raced closer.

Around two weeks later, we got the news we were waiting for – in the shape of another bubble-wrapped medicine bottle of our whisky.

Lining up the panel

We could now book our tasting event at The Scotch Malt Whisky Society in Queen Street, Edinburgh.

We could also confirm our panel – Colin was able to make it, as was Ewan Reid (Matthew Algie's Quality Director) and Dr Eduarda Cristovam – Matthew Algie's sensory analysis expert.

There were also some peculiar coincidences about the makeup of the team. Ewan lived on Islay for many years, and Eduarda had an academic as well as personal interest in Scottish malt whisky.

And, from the tasting notes we'd been supplied, it became clear that the whisky we were working with was Colin's favourite dram.

The tasting night

Our professional tasters were an enormous help. Ewan described the undiluted aroma as "apple, ester, with a tiny bit of lemon at the front of the nose – and leather at the mid-nose". Diluted, he described the nose as "sulphurous, with iodine".

Eduarda felt the undiluted nose had a sweet, honey fragrance – with flowery and vanilla notes. She also noted that the high alcohol content overshadowed the other notes.

Moving on to the taste, Ewan described the undiluted dram as "a semi-anaesthesia", with a well-balanced aftertaste – and Eduarda as

"having your tongue flambéed, but without the pain.

Diluting the whisky, the consensus was of a whisky with a powerful finish – where the strong TCP, wood and iodine notes are nicely balanced with sweet notes.

It's not a dram for the faint-of-tongue.

Ultan and I had some, frankly embarrassing, notes on the whisky. These ranged from "haddock" and "syrup sweetness" to "battery acid" and "orange". Well, I did say they were embarrassing.

Down to work

With a weekend to type up the tasting notes, we met early the following week to start on label concepts. We spent some of the evening simply tasting the remains of our sample – and working through the notes.

We then got talking about some of the lore and legend about Islay, and hit upon the idea of creating our own back-story. There were some elements we really wanted to use: for example, a round church on the island is said to offer no corners in which the Devil can hide. We also wanted to draw on Islay's natural heritage – including the strong maritime tradition.

And above all, we were determined to link our concept right back to the taste of the whisky.

Finding NO WAYWARD SOULS OR SUCCOURING CORNERS, *the Devil* SEARED HIS SCORN INTO THE SWEET *floral* AIR OF THE *island's* NIGHT. AND INTO THIS *precious liquid.*

And then it hit us: the sulphur and fire from the tasting notes could have come from the Devil himself. And the sweetness could be the unspoilt air of Islay. This also links neatly with the Devil's long history in Scottish literature: from the witches' ceilidh in Robert Burns's *Tam O'Shanter* – to James Hogg's *The Private Memoirs and Confessions of a Justified Sinner.*

So we decided to call it an evening: I would create a back-story and some label copy – Ultan would create the visual elements.

Tweaks and twitches

Ultan spent the last weekend before the deadline preparing the final label artwork – as well as experimenting with colours and typefaces. (It took a fair bit of time to get the Devil's tail and horns to work well in the graphic device.)

We'd also discussed re-working my label copy, to see if I could get it to work just that little bit harder. I played about with a few ideas, but nothing was really working – especially as we wanted to fit so many ideas into such a small amount of words. Then I did a quick word count – to discover I'd written precisely 26 words.

After I told Ultan, we both agreed it would be tempting providence to change the copy. So we didn't.

Finding NO WAYWARD SOULS OR
SUCCOURING CORNERS, *the Devil*
SEARED HIS SCORN INTO THE SWEET
floral AIR OF THE *island's* NIGHT.
AND INTO THIS *precious liquid.*

AGED IN OAK – TWELVE YEARS

Single Cask
CASK No. 3.109
SCOTCH MALT WHISKY

Produced in Scotland
BOTTLED BY
THE SCOTCH MALT WHISKY SOCIETY

50cl ℮   60.7% VOL

26

CASK NUMBER

44.29

Ben Braber Ben is a copywriter and communication consultant. Since 1993 he has worked with UK and international business, public and non-profit organisations, helping his clients to find the right words and use them to greater effect. John Tafe John has worked in design and new media for 13 years. Since 1997 he has worked for Front Page Design where he heads up the interactive department, using design and technology to create effective marketing solutions for a wide range of clients.

AN ANGEL CYCLES OVER YOUR TONGUE

Drinking this whisky reminds us of summers at home, that is our homes before we settled in Scotland. John remembers the taste of a refreshing rain shower on a muggy summer night in Boston, Massachusetts, USA. I recall a saying from the part of the Netherlands where I grew up. People use it to describe how well their thirst is quenched: "It is as if an angel is peeing on your tongue." My mother – in an anxious but unsuccessful attempt to protect my youthful ears – puts her own spin on it, replacing the Dutch word for peeing ("piest") with cycling" ("fietst"). We take another look at our glass, noticing again this whisky's extraordinary light and sparkly colour: Heaven's Leak.

This is a summary of our tasting experience.

What struck us most was the colour: light, very pale, mellow with an inviting s...

We both found the taste nothing special: sweet but not to sickly, it also seemed... refreshing, like a summer show... the aftertaste was slightly dark (like burnt woo... hint of bourbon (which ... mind us ... Bazooka Joe chewing gum). After adding taste quickly diminished...

We feel the label should just have the name, perhaps a slogan, image on the obligato... stuff.

You suggested to have a handwritten label, just like the Coren... example ... Dutch... We could go for a peel off label that people can collect labels to ... wind bike? This wo... perhaps differentiate our idea ... in conjunction with the fact that an American and a Dute... man are working on ... Scotch ...

Based on ... The startling ... feature ... the colour, my idea is to call it Heaven's Leak...

The journal would ... story and an image explaining ... peeing on your tongue". label collection ide... The idea for the name de... from ... got to this name and the etc." which my mother prudently chang... as if an angel ... Netherland... Dueth word ... peeing = piest being sub... for ... our memor... Bazooka Joe... mething from our youth. The bourbon ... also ... and the ... wea... of the Sta... nk we should make a lot of our origin... weather ... that was often ... e's

er I thought of our joint experience of the Scotc... journal. g down" could come into play somewhere, f... example ... ill think of images for the label and the journal related to an angel ... refresh... mmer shower and perhaps a cyclist (saying "I'm pissed") ... native would be elegance in relation to the Telford bridge over the river Spey near ery.

s is useful. I will phone you in a couple of days to discuss this further.

ANGEL'S ← WINGS

COLLAGE

' Ye of little faith.

John

Thanks for that. Your label looks really good, beautiful and will get people's attention, but I want to keep the name Heaven's Leak.

As for the typeface, they both work well - you will have to chose. If you want my reactions:
- The traditional is just that. It or a similar font is used by Ardbeg (an Islay whiskey). It gives the whisky weight and a somewhat heavy
- The modern font looks fresh (refreshing like the whisky in the bo is also clean and gives the whisky a lighter character.

Remember that the bottle will be smaller than usual, yet elegant glass.

Do you want to send me a pdf once you have finalised the decor

Then we have have a chat about it early next week. The concept need to be with the SMWS by Friday 3 June.

BIRD, NOT SEAGULL - SMALLER

Hi Ben,

I've attached here some images and designs I've sources as a starting point for designing th whisky label. These are not my designs, but just some research to indicate an initial directi

From these, and the tasting notes, the design would:

LIGHT + REFRESHING

- incorporate a 'summery', light refreshing mood
- use hand writing and/or collage to create a multi layered effect
- incorporate a sense on higher beings (heaven or angels)
- use softer, more effeminate? colours
- remain quite abstract

Let me know you're initial thoughts.

Cheers, *whisky?*
John

HEAVEN'S LEAK

SINGLE CASK SCOTCH MALT WHISKY
cask no 44.29 ✿ aged in oak 11yrs
contents by vol: 50cle ✿ vol: 57.9%

Produced in Scotland
Bottled by The Scotch Malt Whisky Society

26

CASK NUMBER

4.104

Victor Brierley Born Edinburgh (when nobody knew where it was). Agency delivery boy 1981. Then a "suit". Then client PR for six years. Then handling clients, design consultancies, with writing thrown in. Now, client services and stuff at Citigate SMARTS. Black-belt karaoke. George Craigie George set up CRUCIAL in 1997 in Aberdeenshire. He works with clients in a broad range of industries, has attracted a number of awards and is a visiting lecturer at the University of Dundee. Rumoured to sing after a dram or two.

VICTOR'S JOURNAL

It's a REALLY interesting experience, being paired-up with a creative person you've never met. Will you gel? Will your ideas be totally cheesy, or chalky for that matter? Or worse, will you friggin' hate each other? I didn't have to worry because George, in spite of the fact that he was spelling "Whiskey" the Irish way, was looking at this whole project as something which would be fun, enjoyable and not too serious.

We'd also agreed, over a Guinness or five, followed by a couple of rather superior drams in Edinburgh's legendary Port O' Leith bar, that pompous, anal, design-self-indulgence was a no-no. So, a rather great start to any project, by all accounts and although he'll hate me saying this, a great night out, with a thoroughly nice chap.

As George is based up in Laurencekirk, in the North East of Scotland and I'm in Glasgow, in the Central belt, numerous emails came. And went. Most of them containing straight-talking language, far too "Celtic" in content to publish here. All of them were very amusing though. George is a poet … and buddy don't he know it.

Which was good, because I initially had designs on using Frank Sinatra, torch-song lyrics, to portray a "drinker's" whisky. Reflecting on the low-key and even sombre moments, as well as the upbeat nature of enjoying drinking whisky. This was erm … scotched when I read the small print, referring to "original concepts only". The other slightly abstract idea of designing a "Prisoner" whisky, using the tagline "I am

NOT a number!", and assorted imagery and typography (the typeface that featured in the show was called "Village") from the 1960s cult, TV series. As I was only 4 when it was first aired, it's not exactly an original thought, so this was also a non-starter. There was also a wacky, "HP sauce" idea. The least said about that, the better…

So, with my initial ideas as non-runners, we left it for a while. Well, more than a while, whilst everyday design business matters took pride-of-place, in both our studios. Then (and this happened quite a bit) just as I was thinking about 26 again, George called right then and emailed me an idea called "This Way Up". At first, I thought it was a bit too simplistic but then I remembered our (slightly drunken) preamble to approaching the whole project. "Keep it simple, don't produce something too designer pretentious".

It's got legs thought I and I started to keep my bit of the bargain and develop some "words".

It literally came to me by way of my girlfriend, who suggested she knew nothing about where our whisky came from … Apart from a strange thing called the "Ba game", all the locals played at Hogmanay….

A "Eureka" moment if ever there was one, AND it would fit in perfectly with George's "two-glasses" design. Obviously, we're both going to claim the credit for this winning, fun and quirky idea, but like most good ideas, it's been a real amalgam. Also, because I have to, as she'll read this, I've got to mention my girlfriend Pauline. Erm … thanks for all your input!

GEORGE'S JOURNAL

Victor and I got into the swing of things, immediately after the initial introduction. Along with 26-er Iain Valentine, we embarked on some pub visits around Leith – "primary research" – I told my wife. Not the wisest places to enter with a writer, dressed in a dicky bow! However, after the pianos stopped, then started, the banter progressed with the Guinness and we left Leith unscathed, agreeing that we should avoid the heathery, hills & heritage approach – "none of that roamin' in the gloamin' stuff".

So, where to start? Well, to be honest, I didn't do anything until a week before the concept deadline. Lying on my settee, I got to thinking that there is a "dialogue" to be settled with a fine bottle of whisky. The

label speaks to you, seduces you. You, in turn think – will I – or won't I? This "dialogue" idea persisted and I got to thinking about how the bottle is used and how the label's viewed.

The bottle is either upright on a surface, or upside-down on an optic. The drinker is either not drinking, or drinking, up or down. Can we therefore come up with a message and design a label that can work *both* ways, for the position of the bottle and the dialogue between the bottle and the drinker? This was the basis of the brief to myself.

As I started sketching, "THIS WAY UP" was the thought that popped into my head; a nod in the direction of Alan Fletcher, whose witty designs have had a lasting effect on me since college. I then developed a couple of layouts, to get a feel for how it could work. The two glasses in opposition seemed to suggest a Highland dancer, in a kind of Celtic/Runic style. It had possibilities.

The more I thought about the statement, the more it worked for me. It was time to get in touch with Victor to see what he had done and to discuss the way forward. I worked up an Illustrator file of the initial sketch and sent it in an email, which implored: "Any words of wisdom? – attached is my only idea so far – we need to get our finger out!".

Thankfully, we reached agreement – we both liked the concept but Victor would "look" at the words. What then came back was absolutely "on the money". At the top of a list of "possibles" was "UPPIES/DOONIES". As soon as I read it, I saw the typographic solution and it fitted our particular whisky. We had a result!

I made some modifications, mainly to the position, layout and size of the mandatory text, then softened the drawing of the glasses with a "glow" and I rounded the keyline ends. I tried a few colour-ways, and then settled on green and orange as they complemented the whisky colour, in a clear bottle.

I never got to taste our whisky, by the way. The guy in the dicky bow scoffed the lot!

Contents by vol **50cl**

vol **54.6%**

Single Cask Scotch Malt Whisky
Cask No.4 10% **Aged in oak** 16yrs
Produced in Scotland
Bottled by The Scotch Malt Whisky Society

uppies doonies

26 MALTS

CASK NUMBER
64.9

Sarah Burnett Sarah is a copywriter living in Edinburgh. Previous incarnations include being a financial journalist, magazine editor, writing guidebooks to Brussels, being a school matron, and doing a degree in medieval Japanese. **Prem Reynolds** Prem Reynolds is design director at The Big Picture. He is an award-winning designer who loves big ideas and attention to detail. Renowned for his smooth swing, fine palate and...er...his attention to detail.

22 MARCH 2005

SB A whisky tasting at The Scotch Malt Whisky Society. We were told how to taste it, to swirl it, to introduce it to our different taste buds. We also learnt the vocabulary of whisky tasting – a wonderful meeting-place of science and language. Esters, phenols, aldehydes, viscimetry, viscocity. Tints can be gamboges, jonquil; hues can be pellucid, xanthic, umbrous, rubious …

Even the words are intoxicating, particularly when you've spent the morning battling with clients who insist that every sentence contain "leverage" or "delivery".

PR Jumped on a train to Edinburgh with a colleague and spent the trip developing creative for The Macallan. Lunch at Harvey Nics is ideal taste-bud training for the session at SMWS. Great building. Great malts. Great Guinness before heading home.

EARLY MAY

SB I've received my whisky sample for the project. It looks like a TCP bottle; the question is whether it will also taste like TCP. A look at the SMWS map suggests not – it's distillery 64 and therefore a Speyside. A small disappointment. I like the island whiskies that taste elemental, medicinal.

PR To me, whisky has always been a social thing – a dram with friends, a celebration or simply after-dinner-indulgence. I liked the idea of tasting our whisky in different locations. A big swig from a "hipper" on a cold autumn day tastes different to a "home-pour" sitting in front of the fire discussing the latest flob-a-lob.

I talk to Sarah about the idea. We're too busy to meet in Edinburgh so she posts my share. I receive a sample bottle containing a pale, charcoal-ridden liquid and hunt high and low for a thimble big enough to drink from. I give up.

16–18 MAY

SB We finally tasted the whisky. With Prem in Aberdeen and me in Edinburgh, we drank separately. Work, life, logistics were all too complicated for us to manage a joint tasting.

Down in Edinburgh, we thought our sample looked more like a pale fino than a whisky. The aroma was delicate, very much an aperitif whisky. But after leaving it a few minutes, it grew into more of a whisky, developed more character. We tasted grass, a hint of liquorice, burnt toffee, stock that's been cooked too long, flowers, leaves, ink, copper … even remembered eating dandelion leaves as children.

For the fast relief of tir
taste-buds, dull comp
and stilted conversati

DOSAGE

First dram to be taken at leisure.
If symptoms persist, pour another.

PR Distillery 64. Speyside. I crack open the bottle in the studio and pour a keen measure. I nose it. Ouch! I taste it. F***! Is this mouthwash or whisky? I'm left with fresh breath and enamel-stripped teeth. I leave it for over ten minutes and return to a hooter friendly, toffee tainted dram. I taste it again. This time I'm left with a sharp "paracetamol-stuck-on-tongue-from-not-taking-enough-water" taste. I place the lid back on the bottle. Enough is enough.

19 MAY

SB Work begins, via phone and email. We know we want to escape from traditional whisky imagery – so no heritage, no history, no references to where it comes from. One idea is the idea of change – the way that barley and water change into whisky, the way that whisky changes in the cask, in the glass once you've poured it, in your mouth as you savour it, and so on.

But we're also thinking about something much more stark, much further removed from tradition. Maybe just a phrase like "Drink me". Maybe a health warning, along the lines of a food label: "Warning: This product may contain traces of burnt toffee, grass, barley." That way, we could bring in what the malt actually tastes like, as well.

PR Talk to Sarah and brainstorm a few ideas. Suggest losing all cliché whisky imagery and take a different approach. I like the idea of change and wordplay. We discuss the idea of "Warning. May contain traces of toffee etc." I keep coming back to the strong medicinal tastes. The mouthwash, paracetamol aftertaste and TCP colouring.

25–27 MAY

SB I'm becoming frustrated with trying to develop the change theme and the cascading words. It's too similar to the usual whisky imagery of alchemy, the landscape, etc. The size of the label doesn't allow for many words, and it's just going to come out as shorthand and clichés.

While we're thinking about that, Prem mentions that he is still keen on the "clinical" idea of the health warning, and we move to the idea of having a label like a medicine bottle or a prescription: "For the fast relief of …", "For internal use only …", and so on.

I think we're there …

PR Investigate type options/colours with clinical, medicinal feel. We develop the idea of the dram being prescribed. "For the fast relief of…" and tweak the language, changing as many clinical "regulars" to include an element of humour:

- For the fast relief of tired taste buds, dull companions and stilted conversation.
- First dram to be taken at leisure. If symptoms persist, pour another.
- Keep within reach of friends.
- For internal use only.

Finally, I change the orientation of the label to be read whilst pouring the prescribed dose – a dram at leisure. Ideal.

We're there …

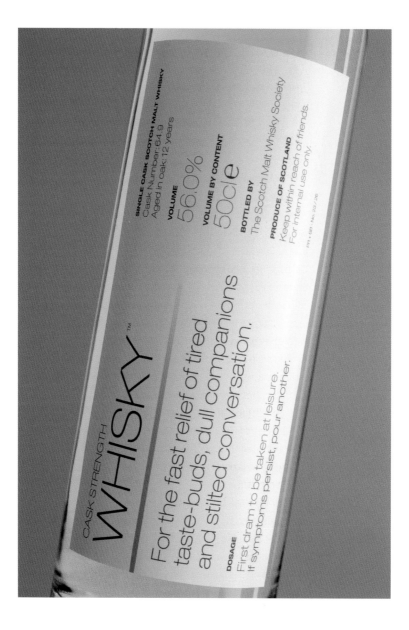

CASK STRENGTH
WHISKY™

For the fast relief of tired taste-buds, dull companions and stilted conversation.

DOSAGE
First dram to be taken at leisure.
If symptoms persist, pour another.

SINGLE CASK SCOTCH MALT WHISKY
Cask Number: 64.9
Aged in oak: 12 years

VOLUME
56.0%

VOLUME BY CONTENT
50cle

BOTTLED BY
The Scotch Malt Whisky Society

PRODUCE OF SCOTLAND

Keep within reach of friends.
For internal use only.

PH • GB • No. 20 / 26

26
MALTS

CASK NUMBER
3.105

Nick Copland Nick ran his own design business in the early 1990s, but quit to become an academic. After a degree in English Language and Literature, and another in Critical Theory, he worked as a freelance writer for six years before joining Elmwood in 2004. **Gillian Thomas** Gillian works at The Partners as a creative consultant. After studying at Liverpool she started her career at Pentagram then worked at Newell and Sorrell, before joining The Partners in the late 1990s.

ANTICIPATION
"Sometimes it is better to travel than to arrive"

MARCH 19TH – TASTING PRACTICE

The tension built gently through the morning as I trundled south through the countryside, then into the ugly back alley of King's Cross. Finding The Scotch Malt Whisky Society added to my sense of foreboding. Despite this – and even wandering like a tourist through the capital gripping my pocket A to Z – I found it quite easily.

Don't mind meeting people, but I was one of the first to arrive. John Simmons turned up too, which was good, as I've met him a couple of times. The half an hour spent upstairs in the boardroom contemplating the three glasses with their precious contents at each place setting on the table added to the pleasant anticipation. Frankly, by the time we sat down and began I was dying for a drink.

Met up with Janet from The Partners – the designer I was to work with. She appeared as inexperienced in whisky as me (which was good) but then explained that she was standing in for Gill who also knew nothing about whisky, to the point that she thought it was spelt with an "e" and it made her shudder when she drank it. So despite meeting Janet, I could still look forward to meeting Gill. More anticipation ...

The tasting over (for which many thanks), I headed off to see my friend Dave who works nearby. He was late—as usual. Couple of pints, then home.

MAY – DELIVERY

Enid Blyton has a lot to answer for in terms of deliveries. Her books are full of cheerful Telegraph Boys with little peak caps who cycle up in the nick of time with a vital delivery, or brown paper parcels tied with hairy string with handwritten labels that would arrive before breakfast and await one alongside one's tea, toast, *Times* and marmalade.

Obviously these are fantasies, and accordingly the delivery of my sample could not have been more different. First I got a yellow card through the door at home. It simply said that some delivery company had attempted to deliver something (they didn't say what) to my home at 11.00am on a Tuesday. I had expected the whisky to arrive at work, so I didn't make the connection – just wondered who was sending me a parcel.

The card said if I didn't claim the parcel, it would be sent back to the sender and I'd have to start again. The gravity of the situation was compounded by the arrival, the next day, of a second yellow card. If this was football I'd have been sent off by now. Perhaps they would send a red one tomorrow.

Finally getting through to the delivery company, I asked them to reroute my sample (for that is what it was) to Elmwood where I could take delivery of it.

Of course I was expecting a small bottle of whisky, but probably not one this small. The slight disappointment was though tempered with excitement – the bottle simply had the Distillery and Cask sample numbers and our names! I couldn't wait to taste it. But of course I did. Wait that is.

Gill had been looking forward to the task ahead too. However, like the whisky itself, the deadline seemed a long way off – she made a mental note – "I don't need to start worrying about this until someone puts a bottle of whisky on my desk!" However when May loomed on the horizon and a couple of emails informed us that the deadline had moved (closer!) she eventually started to get concerned. "No whisky, not met Nick, not sure if I even like whisky, I know the SMWS is near by somewhere, but where exactly? Oh God, I hope Nick can come down to London soon ...."

MAY – THE TASTING PROPER

Another train journey for me, another fabulous sense of foreboding (I'm perversely beginning to relish it now). Arrived at the mighty toilet that is King's Cross, hopped over to The Partners – arrived a little early – sat and waited for Gill.

After a brief chat around our diminutive sample at The Partners, we finally decamped to The Scotch Malt Whisky Society at 4.30pm and were ushered through to a little cubicle with three glasses (were we expected to offer a dram to the barman? Luckily our bottle was far too small for that). The wait was finally over.

ANTICIPATION

IT WAS cool, with a thin layer of
forget a slight scent of lemon. "I
had forgiven me by now," he'd t
Slowly, and almost impercepti
tension was tangible. He knew
without even trying.

He had been expecting this

After a quick look at the tasting handbook – pour, look, smell, taste, just add water, taste again – right let's go – the tasting could begin.

This is what we wrote down: Fleeting, Warm, Knows what it's doing, Consistent, Lemon and honey, Subtle, Pebbles, Seaweed, Sharp, Senses, Young, Not obvious, Peppery, Light, Shy, Optical illusion, Not organic, Citrus, Elusive, Assumed, Slight, Gone up not down, Spring, New buds, Hard to put finger on, Atonement, Earthy, Scientific, Strong yet supple, Trees, Silver birch, Direct, Purposeful, Chemical, Intelligent, Active, Straight, Clean, Skilful, Invigorating, 11.00am–7.00pm, Just before something … , Aperitif, Sharpener, Preface, Anticipation, Memory

Decided to look at a narrative that would somehow build on the sense of anticipation and pleasantly antiseptic functionality of the dram. Perhaps disconnected or incomplete, but well-made and crafted none the less. We decided on a typographic route which would allow plenty of words, and something that would obliquely reference the flavours without being "about" the taste as such.

We talked about a layout that would give clues but not give the game away, leave the reader wanting more, wondering what happens next, completing it for themselves, playing with anticipation and fulfilment and touching on the way we interpret incompleteness. An occluded page that gave the reader narrative glimpses rather than hard facts. This we then did.

SINGLE CASK SCOTCH MALT WHISKY PRODUCED IN SCOTLAND

Aged in oak 12 yrs Cask No. 3.105 Contents by vol 50cl ℮ vol 54.8%

BOTTLED BY THE SCOTCH MALT WHISKY SOCIETY

ANTICIPATION

IT WAS cool, with a thin layer of clo
forget a slight scent of lemon. "I did
had forgiven me by now," he'd told
Slowly, and almost imperceptibly b
tension was tangible. He knew he'd
without even trying.

He had been expecting this to be a
and elusive. Her pale curls were s
She said "All I want is something I
Perhaps because he was a chemis
practicalities. There was simply no
nothing there. It couldn't have been
flickering in the sodium lights. He t
pleasant, but strangely unrewardin
With her cool, thin hands she took
atonement and left him, simply wo
promise left unfulfilled.

The next day he realised what she h

26

CASK NUMBER

3.108

Stuart Delves Stuart co-founded Henzteeth in April 2002 with John Ormston. For the last ten years he has worked extensively for whisky clients including: Highland Park, Glenmorangie, The Glenrothes, Bowmore, Glenfiddich, Black Bottle and The Scotch Malt Whisky Society. **Alan Ainsley** I'm passionate about design and language. Collaboration too, as nobody can have a monopoly on ideas. I've enjoyed seeing my work tattooed on people, the England football crest, but I'd like to believe that we all shared a passion for what we believe in.

STUART

1st nosing – in the bottle – alone – 4th May
(Sneak preview: writer's privilege)

Laundry, chloroform, vanilla
a shifting scent, white pages turning
chlorine on linen gauze
vanilla and iodine; an elusive brackishness

ice cream-cum-shards of brass

2nd nosing – in the bottle – alone – 5th May – Election Day (Sneak 2)

Pale gold in the light; a melted gold bar

A cold coming on or an attack of Hay Fever
Nevertheless, the fumes hit:

A slight haze of alcohol – an echo of sea spray.
I think of liniment: a hero's wounds being dressed by a mermaid.
A spicy, resinous richness
The burnt wood of a barque
Rain-washed oils from a bride's ringlets

Day of results: 1) more of the same 2) something different

3rd nosing – in the bottle – alone – 8th May –
The Sabbath (Sneak 3)

Under the long gaze of the scripture-whispering Hebridean minister I take a sniff through a blocked nose. Linctus – estery balm.

4th nosing – 17th May with Alan Ainsley at The Vaults.
"The Session".

I stride up the stone steps, bottle in pocket. One from The Vaults – a classic West Coast compilation. Pass the whisky round. Roll those laughing bones. Yes, the Candyman's in town.

Alan and I have met once before. Over a Laphroaig. And now, over a Bowmore: distillery no. 3. He and I have established a common ground already: a love of Scotland's West Coast, seafood, elegance, words. To be given a coastal malt – a beneficence. We're amazingly in tune. The label, for me, was painless. What more could I have asked for than a beach-combing, stone-gathering designer, an elfin blacksmith of type. I tell him of a poem I wrote about Islay and Jura: two sisters. He smiled. I share it here as background.

Two sisters
I. Post card
Heart breaks when I leave the west,
The isles in particular
                    Queen
                        Of the Hebrides
        Specifically,
                    Golden sands, wide inlets
                        Daubed with white homesteads
Lapped by blues no fuji no kodak can capture.

Heart dances when I board
                    The ferry,
                            Sail out
                                    Past Gigha
                        And cross the sound to Celtic Heavens
                                        Land
Where the Lords of the Isles landed
                    And drive the long Rhinns to Portnahaven.

Heart stills
With the slow kamikaze
Of sun into Atlantic
Ribboned pink, heather-strewn.
        And as the seals sing
Heralding midnight's
Glassy air
            Star lamps
                    And tinkling rigging
                    You are a thousand miles from tomorrow
                            A thousand blue miles from care.

II. Sound track
But tomorrow comes, even here

And from Port Charlotte Jura
                            Flaunts,   supine like Jane Russell
                    (head flung back, far
            too far

severed mane
　　　the whirlpools of Corryvreckan
　　　　　hungry
for sailors and voyaging princes.)

　　　　　　　Dark sister
On whose brackened hills hinds hide,　　long banished
By some ill remembered pantheon,
　　　　　　Enduring
The beauty of woman the beauty of earth and stone
Where lines and crags catch the heart, where age
　　　　　　　　　Is not decay　　but ever a day.

　　　　　You can imagine
Driving down the single track in grainy black and white
Arriving at the big house, stags' heads loom
In the gloaming hall

　　　And deliciously crafted
Pinewood shadows
　　　Tell the whole story
As you sit down and down
A phenolic dram
Of smoky waters
　　　　　　The lava of peated moors

　　　　　　　　You know
The score　　　　The crippled heiress
Had all her suitors murdered save one

One who played the harp and was blind
And sang of two sisters
One cruel, one kind
Forever bound, their purpose sealed

An older, harder myth
Usurps
The final reel

Published in *Island*, Autumn 2002

ALAN

Discovering that our malt was from the West Coast released some of my happiest memories of times spent on the Westen Isles. In my mind I retreat to where I feel I belong and remember life as it is lived on Harris. Walking on the beach at Scarista, beautiful clear waters, views of the hills of Harris and the Isle of Taransay. The wind, the sun, the icy cold water. We all have memories of those places on earth we would rather be than anywhere else, whenever I find one of those places I pick up a stone, it's my reminder. Holding it transports me to where I want to be.

26

MALTS

CASK NUMBER

41.34

Matthew Fitt Born in Dundee in 1968, Matthew has fished on the Sea of Galilee, slept in Hugh MacDiarmid's bed (he wasn't in it at the time), lived in a Bohemian uranium mining town and currently co-directs a company called Itchy Coo. **Damian Mullan** Hails from County Derry. He studied graphic design at the University of Ulster and the London College of Printing. Moved to Edinburgh in 1993 to work for agencies including McIlroy Coates and Redpath, and founded So... Creative Communications in 2004. He believes everyone has a story worth telling, even businesses.

AIPPLE GUNDIE SUGARALLIE
A Stravaig from Bushmills to Biggar

We'd met a year before, Damian and I, a handshake exchanged in a long Crianza-red boardroom in Edinburgh's New Town.

The assembled company (poets, artists, marketing people) had been supoena'd to appear by a tourism agency, seeking to devise a master plan whose aim was to harass Scots into visiting their own country. Damian to ferment the creative juice was given a fluffy Loch Nessie to cuddle; I had been handed a tartan dolly. The meeting of minds rumbled on towards various conclusions, mine having something to do with Dunadd and the failure of history and too much litter outside railway stations.What Damian's was, I had to wait nine months to learn. We were to meet again in March in another chamber of the Edinburgh New Town barrio at the Malt Whisky Society, a lighter one with a dance floor of a table marked out with glasses and a demonstration model of a process second in age only to the basalt plug of the Castle Rock half a mile to the south. This time they gave us whisky.

Damian and I took to each other in the first shared dram. Although we were meeting in our thirties, both of us married, Damian with a young family, it was as if we were starting school together – whisky school. Damian's northern Irish palette and my east-coast of Scotland nose were the chalk and slate upon which our teacher, Miss Meikle, scratched the words malt, legs, Angels' share. We made meteoric progression from infant toddlers to cynical undergraduates as we were fast tracked towards new vocabulary like fruity, lavender, bicycle saddle, fairy liquid, grannie's *oxters*. This was the tutorial I had not been looking forward to. Years of throwing cushions at Jancis Robinson as she haivered about wine tasting like this or that had hardened me to such folly. But with my nose telling me there was no way other than language, pal, of describing to another human being the sensation offered by a glass of malt and because I found it to be tremendous verbal fun (a fact I kept to myself until I got home and bored my wife into a near coma with), I was soon along with Damian rattling off a litany of abstruse nouns with the best of them.

Our brief was identical to everyone else's – write and design label for whisky bottle – identical in all but one regard: our writing was not going to be in English, but in Scots.

I write in Scots, unashamedly, unconditionally. Scots sounds like *hoose, ken, dreich, scutter, puddock* and *ramiegiester*. If you're wondering if *uisge, feasgar, taigh* and *dubh* are part of this, you've missed the mark by a fair bit and are thinking Gaelic. Think instead about Scots: *kirk, vennel, blate, eemis, gallus, cundie*. This is exactly what Damian Mullan from Coleraine, near Bushmills, in Ulster had to face.

Now my father is Northern Irish and I reckoned I could probably cope with everything Damian threw my way, including any curve balls of vernacular or idiom. Damian for his part has lived in Scotland many years but was a little unsure of what designing for a poet whose work is in Scots might do to his head.

The sample from Dailuaine arrived and I promptly drank most of it. I make my apologies again to Damian, this time in print. I had not realised that the writer was to be given custody of the sole drop of the sample whisky, the only error in judgement I feel on the part of the organisers. (Don't trust writers with free alcohol.)

And so the collaboration began. Sitting together in a bar on a May evening, I smelled *aipples, grozers*, and even a wee bit of *curly andra*.

Damian was getting apples, gooseberries and a hint of coriander. I tasted *gundie*, Damian toffee. We experienced a *snell efterlowe* (a nippy after taste) and both agreed (by this stage Damian enjoying the Scots almost as much as the whisky) that a drop of water sweetened the *craitur* until it was markedly *sugarallie*.

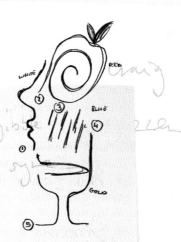

We had our ideas and our text. The hard job was to make a language which is not allowed out of the house these days without stabilisers accessible to imbibers. What if folk don't understand *neibours?* What if they panic after the first *tassie?* This Damian took in his stride as if he'd been brought up in a Cowdenbeath *closie* or the *loans* of Aboyne or the *vennels* of Irvine. He has delivered a subtle design which shows the journey or *stravaig* of words with no recourse to clumsy glossaries or apologetic explanation. And I am immensely proud of it.

For centuries, speakers of Scots have been drinking whisky and using their rich language to describe the experience; Damian and I hope that our *unco, gallus* label will have connoisseurs *bletherin* and *blousterin* as they *weet their gizzen* with this *birsie chiel* of a Speyside malt.

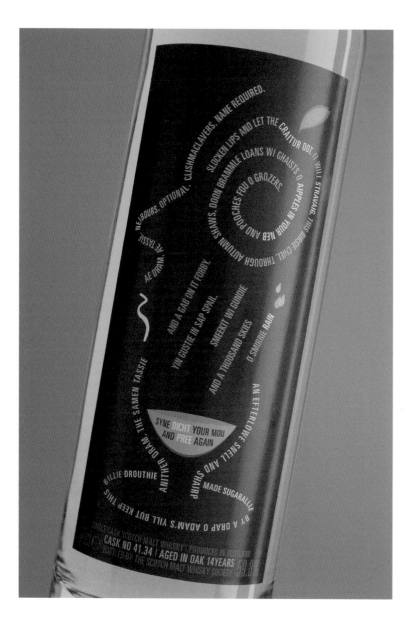

26

CASK NUMBER

122.10

Roger Horberry Roger is a writer and consultant specialising in branding, design and web. He lives in North Yorkshire with Lucy, Lotte and George. In his increasingly rare spare time he makes wilfully obscure music.
Rob Andrews Rob is creative director at R&D&Co, the branding and identity agency he founded with long-time collaborator David Carroll in 2003. He likes to think of his work as thoughtful, innovative and challenging, and is sometimes right.

alookoflemonga
ightaslightoffw
rwaterthenthen
takesholdwarm
over'shuglipsbu
gnumbbeforeth
eetestexplosion
nfectiondetona
lingeringonand
fttoffeefromdi
ocketsbonfiresk
nghotandstrong

Thursday 27 January Do I fancy doing a label for The Scotch Malt Whisky Society? Indeed I do Mr Simmons.

Monday 21 February Got the list of designers today. I'm paired up with Rob Andrews of R&D&Co – ex-Interbrand, Newell and Sorrell. He replies to my email introducing myself with a very complimentary note about my music. Must send him a CD or three – that'll shut him up.

Thursday 10 March To Hatton Garden to the SMWS's London tasting rooms. Just been reading about the history of Hatton Garden in Nicholas Barton's most excellent *The Lost Rivers of London*. Met Rob – he's from York so we had a good chat. A fascinating afternoon being inducted in to the minutiae of whisky by the same woman who did the tasting session in York a couple of years ago with Andy from Elmwood and brother-in-law Leo. Ah, happy days. I always think of whisky as a male drink, but all the tastings I've been to (all three of them) have been led by very knowledgeable women.

Friday 29 April Our whisky has arrived. Pale and interesting. Donning my deerstalker, I see it must be Inchmoan, a well-peated version of Loch Lomond's Inchmurrin single malt, and normally used for blending. It's rare – first bottled for the Limburg whisky festival in 2004 and going for 100 quid a bottle on *whiskyexchange.com*. Lucky old us. The temptation to quaff it all and send Rob some dodgy blend is almost overwhelming.

Thursday 19 May Convinced this must be about sensation – the experience of tasting, not taste as such. The present Mrs Horberry is on holiday in Portugal so I took number one son George to his regular Monday tiddler group and while being ignored by the mums made some useful notes. Partly poetic, partly descriptive. Not sure what that's got to do with anything but it meant I didn't have to talk to anyone.

Friday 20 May Just had a great conversation with Rob. We both agreed we can't possible describe the taste of our whisky in the usual way, but what we can do is describe the feeling of tasting – from sip to taste to swallow to afterglow. Tasting (in terms of the usual SMWS descriptions) is highly specialised, whereas sensation is universal. We may be on to something here.

Tuesday 24 May Just finished our remote tasting session with both of us quaffing away while on speaker phone. Good fun and GREAT whisky. Feeling inspired (and not a little tipsy) I dashed off a poem that mirror the process of drinking – from eye to nose to lips to mouth:

A look of lemon gold
Bright as light off winter water
Then the nose takes hold
Warm as a lover's hug
Lips burning numb
Before the sweetest explosion
A confection detonation
Lingering on and on
Soft toffee from dirty pockets
Bonfires blazing, hot and strong.

But do I have the confidence to go public with this? Course I do. Remember Eno's maxim – "pretentious" should be a compliment not a criticism.

Wednesday 25 May Sent Rob my draft – he's up for it. Quickly sent back visual treatment that really sets the words off, a good example of how design can enhance language. The graduation of colour works a treat in place of word breaks.

Monday 20 June Just seen the final final version – bang on (expect for my typo – ooops). Good old Rob. It's in the bag.

alookoflemongoldbr
ightaslightoffwinte
rwaterthenthenose
takesholdwarmasal
over'shuglipsburnin
gnumbbeforethesw
eetestexplosionaco
nfectiondetonation
lingeringonandonso
fttoffeefromdirtyp
ocketsbonfiresblazi
nghotandstrong

50cle Contents by vol
60.5% Vol

Cask No 122.10
Single Cask Scotch Malt Whisky
Produced in Scotland
Aged in oak 12yrs
Bottled by The Scotch Malt Whisky Society

CASK NUMBER

41.33

Jules Horne Jules is virtual writer-in-residence for Dumfries & Galloway, with a background in BBC radio. She writes plays, nanonovels and stories for the ear and eye, and is currently working on Gorgeous Avatar for the Traverse Theatre. Nina Gronblom Finnish-born Nina is creative director at visual communications consultancy Tayburn, in Edinburgh. She spent the last 14 years working in London, Sydney, Tokyo and Paris. She enjoys jazz, design, jokes, singing, smoking and whisky — preferably all at the same time.

14/05/2005

The Scotch Malt Whisky Society, Queen Street

It's early Saturday night. A trio of girls in small black dresses are rowed on the sofa, waiting to be claimed. They are all, for some unfathomable reason, blonde.

Nina and Ben have arrived to meet our whisky, which arrived in the post in a medicinal bottle with a cracked lid. It's the colour of straw.

"Wee," says Nina. She doesn't mean "small".

No. 7 turns out to be delicate, to the nose and to the tongue. "Fresh," says Nina. "Vanilla."

Already, we're finding a perfume. Ben has "honey" and "biscuit" and "liquorice".

"Sweet and smoky," say I. That might be the effect of Nina's cigarette. Tasters aren't meant to smoke, but Nina has the tongue of an angel. She can nail a flavour at twenty paces. "Camomile, elderflower, champagne."

This is a frisky whisky. "Chiffon, stockings." It's tight on the tongue, like an aperitif. Juices — and words — are flowing. "Fizz, flowers, crème caramel."

CONSE... ...KLIT,
SE... ...UA ...CIDID.
U... UT LA... DO... N GNA
A...GUA, UT ... ...D MINI... HAM,
'LOJI' INH... OI KI...
'K...ST...' ...J...
E...IN... T...
...M... C...NI... ...IE AU
...TE ...W... ...PTI E II
...P/ATE VP/TT L...
...CE...IE... ...NE...
PPICIA DF...
...AT IDT...ATIO
...IM ...O UT PERTFICIA
...TH... ...TE NA JUS CEROE
...KI...ECL...

SINGLE CASK SCOTCH MALT WHISKY

CASK NO. 41.7.
DATE DISTILLED March '90
DATE BOTTLED Feb '04
AGED IN OAK 25 years

Proof 95.3°

Vol 54.5%℮

Contents by vol 50cl

BOTTLED BY THE
SCOTCH MALT WHISKY SOCIETY

"Custard cream biscuits," says Ben. "Coco Chanel," says Nina. "Petticoats, handcream." It seems we're getting ready for a party. As if on cue, the small-black-dress girls unfold their legs and leave for their Saturday night. We're not invited. All across Edinburgh, people are glad-ragging, powder-puffing, zipping and tucking. Nostalgia settles in.

I dab the whisky behind my ears. It's the least I can do.

We arrive at Audrey Hepburn. She has the right mix of minx and melancholy for our growing mood. It's getting dark, and the Edinburghers are out dancing. We're not. Whether it's northern gloom or just plain jealousy, we reach Moon River, and the bitter-sweetness of disappointed dreams. From there, it's a short hop to "deceptive appearances, *trompe l'oeil*, hidden story".

By the time we're ready to go home, our label is pointing towards Jekyll and Hyde – a dose of good old Scots duality. Nina will paint a gorgeous face using typography, and I'll tell her secret sad story.

03/06/2005

Nina sends her first version, using greeked-in text to create the face of Joni Mitchell. It's a perfume label in elegant honey, framed in black – reminiscent of Chanel No. 5, or perhaps a condolence card. And our whisky is No. 7 – another cosmetic connection. The face is ghostly and imperfect close up, but gels into a crystal-clear image from a distance. The text is run together without spaces to create the necessary colour density – a tumble of words.

Joni Mitchell looks a bit down. If the text is melancholy, too, No. 7 drinkers will be sniffing into their drams. We agree to push things in a more upbeat direction.

The concept becomes:

"Our whisky suggests young, lively and delicate – a champagne among whiskies, with a hint of fizz, fruit and floral. It's reminiscent of early evening, of the promise of parties, dances and dresses, rather than end-of-night logfire mellowness.

It's a glad-rag whisky – a going-out, not a homecoming. With its pale looks and sweet spiciness, it wouldn't be out of place in a scent bottle, or dabbed on a wrist.

So, perfume is our inspiration. It's timeless, elegant and memorable, like the young woman who wears it. Our label will draw on perfume design values and suggest an expensive elixir to be savoured and scented, drop for drop."

09/06/2005

Nina inserts an enigmatic Audrey and lifts the background towards yellow. It's become altogether sunnier. The tumble of words suggests stream-of-consciousness. I'm reminded of Molly Bloom's breathless monologue. We decide to play with that: something exuberant about the ordinary joy of a big night out. The words will appear as impressionistic glimpses through the face:

ANDITISSTILLLIGHTANDTHESUMMERNIC
NGTHAHEADPEELINGTHETISSUEFROMT
WCHIFFONLEMONFROTHEROCKANDHOI
OVESSLIPPINGTOGETHERANDHONEYHE
KECHAMPAGNEGLASSSTALKSSUCHEXT
GANCEITOBEDANCEDTORUINONANIG
RTHOFFLOORANIGHTSWORTHOFNOSTAL
IFORTHEFILMSWECOULDSTARINIFWEW
AUTIFULHIMATTHEDOORINTHEGRANDS
HTIEINHANDDANGLINGANDABOTTLI
WSTARTTHESPELLANDTHEKITCHENSPILL
HESFROMTHEHURRIEDTEAWASHINGON
LLEYAWHITECLUTTEROFSHIRTSANDSO
IDUNDERTHINGSATOUREARSLIKECLUM
TKINSHESAYSYOUREADAFFODILTONIC
DZIPSMETIGHTYELLOWUPTHEBACKTILL
FFASHEINTHEDARKPOSHSUITANDUPRIC
KEADANCERANDWE'RETWOPEOPLEMIC
ODENLYTAKEATAXIANYWHEREOANYWH
TALWAYSTOABALLTHERADIOPLAYSANC
CCORDIONANOLDMAN'STUNEFORTAPPI

"And it is still light and the summer nightlength ahead peeling the tissue from the chiffon lemon frothfrock and honey gloves slipping together and honey heels like champagne glass stalks such extravagance! to be danced to ruin on a nightsworth of floor a nightsworth of nostalgia for the films we could star in if we were beautiful and him at the door in a grand suit with his tie in hand dangling and a bottle to start the spell and the kitchen spilling dishes from the hurried tea washing on the pulley a white clutter of shirts and socks and underthings at our ears like clumsy catkins he says you're a daffodil tonight and zips me tight yellow up the back till I'm stiff as he in the dark posh suit and upright as a dancer and we're two people who might suddenly take a taxi anywhere o! anywhere but always to a ball the radio plays accordion an old man's tune for tapping to we hold each other's strange shoulders in the kitchen and sway beneath the socks hands tangled as if they were each others' faster birling faster till we nearly take off into the laundry and fly into the night and afterwards the breath birled right out of me he kisses me a tongueful of whisky that chases into my throat and travels bellywards and out to my skinends where it sits like perfume my breasts all whisky and he asks me would you to say aye my wee daft daffodil and I say aye I will aye."

16/06/2005

The plan was for the text to disappear off the edges of the label, but Nina has worked miracles to weave it around the mandatories, leaving the words whole. We tweak and tuck by email, puzzling out the last few spaces. Every letter counts. Some of the early brainstorm words appear in Audrey's eyes: honey, chiffon, champagne. Nina nudges the face towards a warmer caramel, and that's it. She's good enough to drink.

N°7
SINGLE CASK
SCOTCH MALT WHISKY

BOTTLED BY
THE SCOTCH MALT WHISKY SOCIETY

CASK NO. 41.33
AGED IN OAK 14 YEARS

50cl   60.4%vol.

PRODUCED IN SCOTLAND

26 MALTS

CASK NUMBER

37.26

Jamie Jauncey Having told stories for The Macallan and Rémy Martin, Jamie likes fierce spirits almost as much as he likes words. A novelist and musician, he was an adult before he discovered that not everyone sees letters, names, dates and numbers in glorious technicolour. **Lucy Richards** Lucy runs StudioLR, one of Scotland's most notable design agencies. A masters design graduate of ECA, and previously with Imagination in London and McIlroy Coates in Edinburgh, Lucy started the business in 1996 and has built a reputation for the highest level of creativity, reliability and commitment.

JAMIE'S JOURNAL

"Do you know about synaesthesia?" asked Lucy.

We were deep in club chairs in The Scotch Malt Whisky Society's huge, high-ceilinged room in Leith. We'd already been sniffing, tasting, ruminating for an hour or so; reaching, sometimes with difficulty, for the words and images to describe the sensory experience.

We'd noticed that our whisky had no "legs", those viscous teardrops of alcohol that usually run down the inside of the glass, and we'd toyed briefly with the idea of naming it "Legless". We'd turned to landscape, and this had conjured up waving barley for Lucy, freshly cut stubble fields for me, and those big cylindrical bales of straw for both of us ...

My only previous experience of this kind had been, at best, a quasi-collaboration with a legendarily talented but geographically remote partner (he was in London, I was in Scotland). His preferred means of communication was handwritten fax and we never met throughout the whole project.

But I'd already met Lucy at the 26 Malts introductory tasting session. She'd struck me as a warm, down-to-earth sort of person and I knew this partnership was going to be real. Nevertheless, I was afraid that once we got together we might not gel creatively, or we might loathe the whisky, or I might not be able to find the words I wanted.

And now here she was asking me if I knew about synaesthesia. I could feel the hairs stand up along my forearms.

"Yes, I do," I replied. "I have it. And you?"

She nodded.

We looked at each other.

Synaesthesia occurs in about one person in two thousand. Although it tends to be more common among people who are creative, the odds of two out of a group of fifty-six being synaesthetic are nevertheless pretty long; and of those two then being paired off together, a lot longer still.

A kind of glitch in the neural circuitry, synaesthesia is the result of separate sensory centres being accidentally wired together. So synaesthetes may experience sounds or tastes as colours, smells as shapes, or most commonly, as in Lucy's and my case, words and letters, names and numbers as colours – though not the same colours.

As we began to explore our synaesthetic palettes, the theme of straw seemed to gain momentum. Lucy sees her own name as a kind of straw-gold colour (for me, "Jamie" is red); while I see the number six, the sample number of our whisky, in a similarly strawlike hue. As for the distillery number, thirty-seven, Lucy sees both the numbers three and seven as a vivid emerald green.

So we had a name, Emerald Straw. We also had the makings of a code with which we could shroud our creation in layers of delicious obscurity. And we had a nice metaphor for the whisky-tasting process itself, a synaesthetic experience if ever there was one, combining as it does the senses of smell, taste and texture.

There was one final discovery still awaiting us, like the warming moment when the whisky reaches the pit of the stomach. Lucy mentioned to me that she lives in Breadalbane Street in Edinburgh. I live on the very edge of the ancient district of Breadalbane in Highland Perthshire and my children go to Breadalbane Academy.

So it was obvious that Lucy and I, united by our weird but life-enriching condition, should collectively – and happily – become Breadalbane Synaesthesia. As for the rest, it's all (including our names) on the label …

LUCY'S JOURNAL

I'm so looking forward to this project, see you soon.

Have been laid out with flu for three weeks, but our whisky hasn't appeared yet anyway so nothing lost on this particular score . . . OK on Wed 4th May for our creative bonding (!) session?

What did we say we'd do, lunch, dinner?

We could start with lunch …

The package has just arrived - looks like a small bottle of pee!

That was fun. I'm going to mull things over, sip some more no. 37 and we'll see what happens.

Some random ideas that have been swirling about in my head. First a haiku:
LEGLESS
Long legs are not the
Only sign of alcohol
Thank God. This had none.

Name – I couldn't find the green agricultural word we hoped for, and all the other green words seem too suggestive of the thing they describe …

If emerald really is the synaesthetic colour closest to your numbers, then that's what we should go with.

Here is my first shot at the label. It's a little sparse. It needs to be richer with some depth. I have been selective with your words but you must be happy with my choice so do let me know what you think and I can swap, or add, or remove.

I've added in two more words to replace the obviously whisky ones, which I hope you like … you'll see more clearly how they're supposed to make a poem of sorts with a structure, rhythm and some rhyming - all of which I'd like to keep if at all possible: fresh stubble sharp strong smooth warm spikey blond mousy musty fine shiny sweet raw emerald straw. The McGuffin – you were right, it's the significant detail!

Here is my latest. I wonder if we lost the bar chart names whether we could make the "strapline" A RARE BLEND OF NUMBERS & COLOURS (no "words"). This doesn't allow the poem to be part of our blend – was that part of the "words" or was that relating to the names? Oh I'm confused now. I'll keep at it.

This is getting better all the time Lucy! One or two more suggestions for bar treatments and a new McGuffin on the attached sheet. And could you possibly shunt "fresh" to the left a bit so it sits bang across the 12 o'clock position and is obviously the first word to read in the circle?

OK, good idea about the finer barcode. Looking better all the time. Do you like me being "Breadalbane" (I live in Breadalbane St).

Is it all getting a bit too busy in the bottom half now? Could we balance it better by reversing the barcodes so I'm left, you're right (which is also alphabetically correct)? I do like Breadalbane. My kids go to Breadalbane academy in Aberfeldy!

"Realised by" says a few things to me (good things) including the realising that we both have synaesthesia. "Breadalbane Synaesthesia" seems more interesting than society or team or whatever, it sounds like a unique condition peculiar to Breadalbane. Which it is. Because we are. It would make a good title for a research paper.

I think you've cracked it! Only one thing missing, now Cask no: 37.6. The thirty-seven gives you your emerald and the six gives me my straw – yes?! And we've missed out a line: Single Cask Scotch Malt Whisky.

OK will put that in. I'm sure it was in there at some point … must discuss our "story" submission too?

And we did. And this was it.

sweet raw emerald straw fresh stubble sharp strong smooth warm spiky blond mousy musty fine shin

Emerald Straw

A RARE BLEND OF WORDS, NUMBERS & COLOURS

VOL: 59.9%

CONTENTS BY VOL: 50cl e

SINGLE CASK SCOTCH MALT WHISKY
CASK NO: 37.26 AGED IN OAK: 18 YEARS
BOTTLED BY THE SCOTCH MALT WHISKY SOCIETY
PRODUCED IN SCOTLAND

REALISED BY BREADALBANE SYNAESTHESIA

26

CASK NUMBER

55.15

Martin Lee Martin keeps the wolf from the door by helping brands remain true to themselves and relevant to their customers, hopefully at the same time. This allows him to indulge his loves of family, books, football and bad puns. Jeremy Scholfield With over 20 years in the design industry under his belt, 17 of them with Newell and Sorrell and Interbrand, Jeremy finally founded a company of his own last year. Skin (ultimate packaging, of course) is based in Chelsea.

MARTIN'S JOURNAL

Friday 29 April

Strange. Not expecting a courier. What's he got? Rip open the medically white Jiffy bag. Still thinking medicine when a small bottle drops into my hand, with a liquid the colour of pale straw inside. There are also unwholesome black specks inside and there's a white label on the other side of the bottle. A moment of instant confusion and severe distaste. Is this some diseased urine sample that's been wrongly delivered? Think momentarily of Queen Mary's Hospital just up the road in Roehampton. Turn the bottle round to see that it is a sample, but a sample of single cask malt for Jeremy Scholfield and me to draw inspiration from in the design of our label. Suspect that my first thoughts should be put to one side.

Saturday 30 April

The label on the sample is suitably enigmatic. Distillery: 55, Sample No: 12. Try shaking it. There are more black specks than I'd first realised. It looks like a post-modern version of one of those snowstorm paperweights that your Auntie Muriel always brought you back from Morecambe or Torquay.

Wednesday 4 May

First meeting with Jeremy. We meet at his office near the King's Road. Neither of us can quite cope with the surreal nature of having a lunchtime whisky tasting in a room that is set up for business meetings. We haven't been given enough of the sample to allow the whisky to do what whisky does best and put us at our ease. We also know that we have to pay especially close attention if we are to make any decent rendition of the contents into words and design. The tutorial we were given a few weeks back had generous lashings of whisky associated with it, and as a result, nearly all the advice about nosing and swirling and so on has leaked away ...

Despite its unpromising look, the whisky is a joy. Much more mellow and reserved than the big bruisers I normally go for – the musclebound Islays all dressed up as nightclub bouncers.

Weekend of 7 and 8 May

We'd quickly realised that we had to move away from orthodox whisky tasting language. During our meeting we'd discussed about four possible routes, but only two of them were worth even beginning to develop. One involved the personality of the whisky talking in the first person, stimulated by the idea of "it's the whisky talking" and the other being two characters in dialogue over the dram in question. At this stage I was open minded about which was the better approach.

The
Chattering Glass

"Wonderful, wouldn't you say? Young, in the prime of life." **"Superb. Clean, smooth, reminds me of late spring or early summer."** "But not brash." **"Good heavens, no. Calm and relaxed."** "Yes, quite at home with itself, not at all showy or arrogant." **"Definitely more Jean Muir than Vivienne Westwood."** "More Kirsty Wark than Jeremy Paxman." **"Very good. There is something slightly feminine about it, but with a hint of sharpness in there too."** "What footballer would it be? Georgie Best?" **"No, the silky skills are there, but altogether too obvious. Somebody equally effective, but more...understated. Denis Law."** "It's like the kind of person you don't notice at first, a brilliant host at a party..." **"Never the centre of attention, but great at giving you a warm welcome."** "Self-effacing, but making their presence felt gradually." **"Another dram?"** "I thought you'd never ask." **"I couldn't get a word in."**

Monday 23 May

Meet up again at Jeremy's office. Brought what was left of the whisky sample with me, but even I haven't descended to drinking whisky at 9.30 on a Monday morning. We did have a bit of a sniff though. Or nose, if that's more proper.

Jeremy had done three routes, all of which were fascinating, two of which were superb, and one of which was just simply the one. It didn't take long to agree that the chattering glass was the best way forward. It captured so much: the dialogue itself, the whisky glass and the characters economically combined in one image together with their conversation, and even the echo of the idea of two people in collaboration, meeting around a whisky.

JEREMY'S JOURNAL

I'm slightly late for the tasting induction and out of breath from the stairs at Greville Street. Luckily there are a few faces I recognise in the room at the top and this helps settle the nerves. Apart from being reassuring, the reunion with some old friends helps me to truly immerse myself in whisky culture later on in the members' bar. In fact I probably submerge myself with one or two drams too many and I'm the last to leave. I start writing down my design thoughts on the train home to Haslemere. The words flow (something I've always found with good malts) but the next day I find little of my writing to be intelligible.

Martin phones to arrange a get together so we can sample the sample and discuss some ideas. We agree on Wednesday lunchtime. I cancel meetings for that afternoon.

I have a number of ideas before our get together. All of them involve depth and strength of colour. As soon as I see our sample I know it's back to the drawing board. It's not dark and peaty, but light and airy although it does have hidden depths when we taste it, a bit of a split personality. Martin and I have a good chat and the malt gets the senses going, although we could have done with more (it really was that good and both Martin and I are fans of malts). By the end of the session we have come up with two or three interesting ideas to work on.

Martin soon produces some copy that beautifully captures our discussion and the ideas on the character of our whisky. I want the design to be simple and elegant — a way of bringing Martin's words to life and letting them do the work. I experiment with a couple of different graphic ideas. One is based on the idea of the whisky itself talking. I think about speech bubbles and quotation marks, but then remembering my writing on the train, I wonder how the words would look if they were brought to life on the label, gradually becoming less intelligible under the influence of the malt.

The other idea is a dialogue, a conversation between two people about the character of the taste. I experiment with the text weaving a pattern on the label. I want it to be like a tartan. It's starting to work, but I prefer another idea, the words hanging in the air between two people defining them and painting a picture of the malt itself.

When Martin and I meet up to discuss the designs a couple of weeks later, we are both confident that the latter is the best. We really like the way it captures the spirit of the project too.

Martin comes up with a great title, revises the copy to help me define the shapes better and a few days later the label is done. A truly enjoyable experience and I can't wait to buy a bottle with our label on it.

The Chattering Glass

"Wonderful, wouldn't you say? Young, in the prime of life.""Superb. Clean, smooth, reminds me of late spring or early summer.""But not brash.""Good heavens, no. Calm and relaxed.""Yes, quite at home with itself, not at all showy or arrogant.""Definitely more Jean Muir than Vivienne Westwood.""More Kirsty Wark than Jeremy Paxman.""Very good. There is something slightly feminine about it, but with a hint of sharpness in there too.""What footballer would it be? Georgie Best?" "No, the silky skills are there, but altogether too obvious. Somebody equally effective, but more…understated. Denis Law.""It's like the kind of person you don't notice at first, a brilliant host at a party…""Never the centre of attention, but great at giving you a warm welcome.""Self-effacing, but making their presence felt gradually.""Another dram?" "I thought you'd never ask.""I couldn't get a word in."

vol 58.4%

contents by vol 50cle

Single Cask Scotch Malt Whisky
Produced in Scotland
Bottled by The Scotch Malt Whisky Society

Aged in oak 11 years
Cask no
55.15

26

MALTS

CASK NUMBER

77.10

Karen McCarthy Karen writes everything from jacket blurb, web copy and press releases to radio drama and poetry. She runs her own communications consultancy, is the editor of two literary anthologies and is currently writer-in-residence for Spread the Word. **Chris Harrison** Chris Harrison spent 12 years at some very grown up design agencies (with nice sofas) before committing career suicide by setting up his own design agency (from a dusty sofa) in Brighton. He plans to take on work, in return for payment, very soon.

WE WENT TO A BAR TO SAMPLE OUR WHISKY

.....WITH OYSTERS

CHRIS EATS AN OYSTER

KAREN AND CHRIS DOWN THE OYSTERS

....AFTER A WEE DRAM

'Just a wee dram,'
I said.
How was I to know a
single cask Scotch malt
whisky straight after breakfast
would make me feel quite
so deliciously frisky?
It slipped down my throat,
lithe and luxurious
as an oyster
before lunch.
I was surprised,
pleasantly, by the fire
that came
later.
Hot sunshine
hit the back of my tongue
and I have to confess
it was heavenly.
'Another?'
Well, who was I to say
anything but yes!
There was something
irresistibly risky
about the whole affair.
This was one unforgettable
afternoon.
Of course, nothing lasts forever,
particularly not the best
things, and before I knew it,
I lifted my glass
and realised, once again,
it was
time for some more whisky!

CASK No. 77.10
SINGLE CASK SCOTCH MALT WHISKY AGED IN OAK FOR 17 YEARS
PRODUCED IN SCOTLAND BOTTLED BY THE SCOTCH MALT WHISKY SOCIETY

Contents by vol 57.6% Vol 50cle

26

CASK NUMBER

24.86

Aird McKinstrie

Aird McKinstrie
Born in '56 in equatorial swelter –
Port Harcourt on the Niger Delta.
Education varied, never thorough,
Completed school in Edinburgh.
Art School – Gray's in Aberdeen,
Staff tolerant but hardly keen.
Illustration has maintained sanity,
Worldwide clients help his vanity.

Prologue and apology

I should begin this essay by explaining that there are not two people on the planet (that I'm aware of) with the unlikely name of Aird McKinstrie and that the reason I have ended up in the unfairly privileged position of doing both bits of this contribution is due to a rare piece of misadventure.

I began the exercise, like all the other designers involved, paired randomly with a writer. Unlike all the other designers my writer decided that we could not work together or rather that the way that we had decided to move ahead (due to work pressures etc.) did not work. Enough said, I think.

Being late in the day for alternative writers to rescue me I have given both roles my best shot, I'm sorry it bends the rules but I've tried to stick to the spirit of the experiment. Besides, with all the sample whisky drunk, it would have been a tall order even for the most eloquent of authors.

Writing

I felt that, in the circumstances, the best course of action was to go back to the beginning and (my notes being back of a fag packet stuff) try to assemble as clear a recollection of the tasting as possible.

The pad that I had scribbled on contained just three words; pucker, midges and water. Not very helpful or auspicious. However one of these words made it through the audition because I recalled that my very first reaction to the neat malt had been confusion with the swarming flavours.

At the time of the tasting there had been discussion about trying to find a descriptive route to the sensory impressions beyond tastes and I still found that intriguing, particularly as my interpretation of other whiskies has often varied from accompanying notes and it seemed unfair to burden people with the expectation of aniseed or jet fuel because of my nicotine and caffeine addled tongue. I know this argument is flawed by the sheer fact that my words proceed to try and give some clue to the drinking experience but I have tried to describe the total experience rather than draw out detail.

Another lasting impression from my first encounter with this malt was the radical transformation when water was added, not uncommon, I know, but here it changed a challenging drink into a relaxing one and I have tried to convey this contrast.

The third characteristic of this malt that I decided to try to allude to was the mood that it created, I had been struck by the attraction of drinking it neat, early in the evening, late in the year when its warmth would be welcome and comforting, yet when water was added it seemed ideal on the bright summer evening when I test drove it.

So that is where the words came from – two different drinks in one bottle and a sense of time – the decision to try haiku came from my own pretension but seemed apt given the poetic nature of whisky and the space limitations of a label.

Design

When I took my first drink of whisky surreptitiously from my dad's supply (never lasted long enough to merit a cocktail cabinet, even though it would have sounded good) I fell in love with it, but what struck me straightaway was how modern it tasted – rough, crowded with experiences and immediate, like city life. Okay that's all post-rationalised, at fifteen I just thought "modern".

The sense has never left me and I've always felt that the commercial adherence to tradition in whisky labelling was a shame, no matter how hard it has been driven by market research. So in the heady circumstances of a client-free (apologies to the Society) experiment I felt that the inappropriate would be appropriate.

The fact that I had given myself haiku to deal with suggested a Japanese lack of symmetry and I will confess to enjoying the irony of adapting some of their styling for our national drink since they have done so well at adapting it to their requirements.

Colour was an easy decision, at the tasting I had felt that the neat drink tasted purple, I don't know why but it tied to the mood of the words and is as close to the complementary colour to whisky as you can get. This was probably the only element from my initial work with the writer that survived unchanged and is still the one element that I'm scared may not be right. That in itself may be a good enough reason to try it but others will have to judge it now.

Typography is never as easy as it seems. On an end product if it draws too much attention away from the sense of the words it has failed (that's my view – not always fashionable) so I wanted to keep things simple. Two levels of communication – informational and subjective description – so two levels of type. Obvious choices for both I suppose, script makes it clear that an individual voice is being expressed and helps the pauses in short text with a specific metre and a clean no-nonsense sans serif for the business stuff. With the statutory information I have tried to be inclusive and let them contribute to the overall design rather than tuck them away and minimise the damage as is often their fate.

The Illustration is another conceit – who would expect insects on a bottle of whisky? The Japanese?

SINGLE CASK SCOTCH MALT WHISKY
Aged in oak 20yrs
Produced in Scotland
Cask No 24.86
Neat;
A mouthful of midges.
Downloads autumn
sweet and slow,
then evaporates.
Water clarifies;
cereal clues
flit fast,
like dragonflies
on broadband.
Vol 55.2%
Contents by vol 50cl e
BOTTLED BY THE SCOTCH MALT WHISKY SOCIETY

26 MALTS

CASK NUMBER

3.110

Charles MacLean Charles established MacLean Dubois (Copywriters) in 1976. He wrote his first leaflet for the whisky industry in 1981. Since then he has published eight books on the subject. He has chaired the Nosing Panel of The Scotch Malt Whisky Society since 1993. **Graham Scott** Creative director of Nevis Design in Edinburgh, Graham studied at St Martins and Glasgow Schools of Art. Clients include: Adelphi Distillery, Hamilton & Inches, Lyon & Turnbull, Freeman's of Philadelphia, Highland Spring and The Royal Bank of Scotland.

THROUGH THE LOOKING GLASS

We enter a white room, a *tabula rasa* – perhaps John Updike's white sheet of paper, "radiant as the sun rising in the morning", or Kandinsky's freshly sized canvas, "pregnant with all possibility".

We find it unnerving, but not unduly ominous. We have been in similar rooms before. There is a profound silence here; the temperature is neither hot nor cold; the atmosphere, at least to begin with, is not oppressive, even when the door by which we have entered merges with the white wall. There are no windows, and although the room is bright, no immediately discernible source of light. An operating theatre comes to mind, and this sets going a butterfly-tremble in our guts.

Inevitably, our attention is focused upon the glass which stands alone on a white table in the middle of the room. Mercifully, bearing no similarity to an operating table. It is a tulip glass, a bulbous copita, and contains what looks like *vin gris* – a pale liquid, the colour of tarnished silver shot with lime, glittering in the even light. Beside it is a flask of water.

yoos

‘whit
vant?’

We take up the glass and sniff. The physical sensation is both peppery and nettley. Then the visions begin ...

The room is now a kitchen. On a formica dresser is an Arbroath smokie, half unwrapped from its waxed paper packet. A pan of gooseberries is bubbling on the stove. The sink is full of dirty dishes and very soapy hot water, and the scent from this mingles with a background of artificial air-freshener.

A large, raw-boned, somewhat ill-kempt woman in her thirties is cleaning a window with a cloth soaked in spirituous cleaning fluid which smells of vinyl and antiseptic. The cloth squeaks across the glass ...

To clear the mirror, as it were, we take a sip from the copita. The flavour is very hot – at once fiery and spicy and etheric – Fisherman's Friend lozenges. Aggressively acidic and salty, with distant diesel fumes. We hastily add water.

Now we are observing a fishing boat, moored alongside a pier. The boat's diesel engine is running and puffing grey smoke. In a moment, we notice it is not only the engine that is making smoke: the woman we encountered earlier is now reducing seal blubber in a pot over a brazier, which she is stoking with bits of tyre and animal bones. She is wearing a Burberry baseball cap and a PVC apron. Fishing nets lie on the deck, with the dry remains of prawns and crabs entangled in them. Bladder-wrack clings to the pier, whispering.

Seaweed imbues the flavour of the liquid – iodine and operating theatres; a taste which begins sweet, becomes acidic and salty; a texture at once oily and *spritzich*, as if the seaweed had been sprinkled with cayenne pepper. Smouldering tractor tyres still linger in the mouth, and our final vision is of a friendly, Burberry crowned, face saying:

"Whit yoos want?"

Single-Cask Scotch Malt Whisky
[SMOKE AND MIRRORS] **Produced in Scotland Bottled by The Scotch Malt Whisky Society Cask No: 1.110 Aged in Oak: 12 years**

This is not a bottle, it's a mingle packet. A pan of gooseberries is bubbling on the stove. On a formica unit there lies an Arbroath smokie, half unwrapped from its waxed paper. A cloth soaked in spirituous air-freshener. A large, raw-boned, somewhat ill-kempt woman in her thirties is cleaning the glass. To clear a window with a background of artificial air-freshener. The sink is full of dirty dishes and very soapy hot water, and the scent of the mirror - as it were - we take a sip. The flavour is very hot – at once fiery and spicy and etheric – Fisherman's Friend lozenges. Agressively acidic and salty, with distant diesel fumes. We hastily add water. Now we are looking at a fishing boat moored alongside a pier. The boat's diesel engine is running and puffing grey smoke. Then we notice it is not only the engine that is making smoke. the woman we encountered earlier is now reducing seal blubber in a pot over a brazier, which she is stoking with bits of tyre and animal bones. She is wearing a Burberry base-ball cap and a PVC apron. Fishing nets lie on the deck, with the dry remains of prawns and crabs entangled in them. Bladder-wrack clings to the pier, whispering Sea-weed imbues the flavour of the liquid – iodine and operating theatres; a taste which begins sweet, becomes acidic and salty; a texture at once oily and spritzich, as if the sea-weed had been sprinkled with cayenne pepper. Smouldering tractor tyres still linger in the mouth. Our final vision is of a friendly, Burberry crowned, face saying:

yooswant?' **'whit**

Vol 63.6% 50cl ℮

26

MALTS

CASK NUMBER

2.63

Richard Medrington Director of Puppet State Theatre Company, Richard is a veteran of eleven Fringes, an Edinburgh Poetry Slam Champion and was shortlisted for the Creative Scotland Awards, 2003. Poet, playwright and animator, he is the only puppeteer from Scotland to have performed solo at the National Theatre. **Chris Allen** Born Midlands, '60s, homemade clothes. Educated '70s, '80s, bad hair and music. Degree multi-disciplinary design. London 11 years, good music, food, clothes — employed, self-employed, employed. Edinburgh late '90s, married with two, hair?, fashion?, creative director at Designlinks. Upright and happy.

RICHARD'S JOURNAL

My father was a wine merchant in Liverpool and at one-time President of the Wine and Spirit Association of Great Britain. Shortly after his death last year I decided to join the SMWS. He never visited the place, but every time I go to the Vaults in Leith I imagine him sitting by the fire, in his element, bulbous nose hovering over a slowly oscillating glass.

On hearing of the 26 commission my first act was to write the following:

"MEDICINAL PURPOSES"

In case of toothache
my Father would bring
an eggcup full of whisky
up to my room,
not for drinking but
for rubbing on the gums.
I remember how pleasingly
my gum-flesh squeaked
and the drowsiness

entering my bones,
but most of all our small
unspoken alliance
against the might
of Mother's abstinence.

I used to have toothache
quite often in those days.

I sit at my desk and contemplate the medicine bottle with its pale yellow contents. I pour a small amount into a glass and watch it cling to the sides. The aroma is summery – I'm relieved to find none of those slightly worrying overtones of Airfix modelling glue. Instead I think of harvest time, of an old man contentedly mowing a camomile lawn, honeybees buzzing and, somewhere nearby, a Golden Retriever lying on its back with its legs in the air.

As I breathe in the scene more deeply the power of the spirit burns my nostrils – summer has a kick, the bees sting, the dog has teeth, the lawnmower can suddenly slip into gear and drag you into a flowerbed.

Before I get around to actually tasting the whisky, the first draft of a poem has pretty much written itself. On closer inspection the four verses each turn out to be within a whisker of the classic haiku format. A little tweaking and they all have the requisite 17 syllables. The seasonal theme is also appropriate, though the inclusion of metaphor and rhyme would not appeal to the haiku purists. Still, I like the simplicity of the form – not too many adjectives.

I wonder about the childhood associations, yet this seems right for a drink which is in a sense the ultimate distillation of the harvest, evoking those concentrated, wrong-end-of-a-telescope kind of memories: holidays in the countryside in a distant past when summers were baking hot and the sky was always blue. I look up the word "genius" which has somehow elbowed its way into the last verse and refuses to budge. Most of the definitions mention the word "spirit". This too seems appropriate.

I pass on my results and the bottle to Chris Allen. He likes the poem and his memory banks produce the image of his grandfather's garden shed – the summer sun has heated it up and released the latent smells of warping wood, of grass clippings …

The mower starts first time. He lets in the clutch and we're away.

CHRIS'S JOURNAL

It's very rare to be asked to interpret a product with such an established generic identity – too good an opportunity to be missed.

The tastings at the Vaults were an eye opener and suggested that the task in hand was going to be more complex than I had first thought. Visually describing a conclusion didn't concern me but identifying the right "notes" did. Following that introduction, I kept away from excessive whisky tasting and stuck to picking the flavours or ingredients out of food – slightly easier.

Any concern I had about the "notes" disappeared when our malt arrived – a light, green, subtle malt with plenty to describe. The process was made easier by my partner's ability to weave a story whilst leaving enough spaces. With the haiku we had structure, atmosphere, light and shade. There was also a very personal thread running through the words which, for me, brought it to life.

Finding a place where all of these described flavours came together was easy and took me back to my own childhood. A warm sunny place where old smells blended together: where furniture had been made, over-wintered fruit wrapped in newspaper, paint, oils and things stored in jars, garden machinery cleaned and stored and the odd bottle from Christmas kept. It's somewhere I still escape to – Pop's shed.

SUMMER SONG Sunshine fades the fields –
a golden retriever roaming
home through the grain

Out with the old *Atco*
time to mow and roll
the lawn before it rains

Summer gives you a punch
on the nose and shackles you
with daisy chains

Childhood caught in a
magic bottle – let the genius
loose again!

SINGLE CASK SCOTCH MALT WHISKY
CASK NO. 2.63
AGED IN OAK 16yrs
Vol 59.8% ℮
Vol 50cl ℮
PRODUCED IN SCOTLAND
BOTTLED BY THE SCOTCH MALT WHISKY SOCIETY

26 MALTS

CASK NUMBER

53.92

Chris Miller Chris is a teetotal freelance copywriter based in Edinburgh. By the time this book's printed, he'll have turned 40. If a midlife crisis ensues and he turns to drink, he'll probably select the wonderful malt he's been working on. Susanna Freedman Susanna has over ten years' experience in the design industry. After returning from working in the US in 1998, she founded her own agency, Tsuko. She was just 22. Younger than many of the malts she's downed at The Scotch Malt Whisky Society.

JOURNAL: 11 JULY 2005

Despite what judges may have said to French defendants in WWII war trials, isn't collaboration great?

The first time the two of us met was at the initial briefing/nosing/sipping session at the SMWS in Leith. Which was a gloriously civilised way to spend an afternoon.

Disappointingly, neither of us could claim to be the much-needed whisky buff of the team. Each hoped the other would be a tweed-clad, bulbous-nosed aficionado. Yet we managed not to disgrace ourselves: neither of us drank straight from the bottle; nor did we suggest that adding a drop of 7-Up would do wonders for any of the venerable malts.

We even managed to affect looks of self-confidence and wisdom when all around us looked genuinely in their element. Particularly the tweed-clad, bulbous-nosed ones.

Annabel, our charismatic host, really knew her onions. Which, weirdly, seemed to be the only foodstuffs her frighteningly perceptive palate failed to detect hints of in the various malts she set before us.

We both left the session having been educated and entertained. And we chuckled in the knowledge that the artwork deadline was but a distant speck on the horizon. In fact, in neither of our careers had we ever had such a wonderfully relaxed lead-time.

But the weeks soon evaporated like the *angels' share* from an oak cask (yes, we now converse entirely in whisky-related similes). And a hint of panic set in. But, mercifully, it was quickly followed by a few crucial eureka moments.

Fine so far, then. Unfortunately, there were to be a few elephant-sized flies in the ointment.

1) Susanna's email system kept crashing, courtesy of BT. Oh, what fun we had thinking up alternatives to "British" and "Telecom" for those initials.

And even when the system was up and running again, it vindictively and inexplicably singled out Chris's email address as the only one on the planet to which it would not communicate.

WHISKY

This is actually an exquisite Scotch malt. It has a slight mustiness and saltiness, together with a lip-smacking combination of Jamaican ginger cake and honeyed malt beer. So we thought you'd appreciate us deterring your guests from trying it. Simply place the bottle on a shelf sufficiently high that they're only able to read the large type. Slàinte!

2) Chris went away on a three-week holiday.

The holiday didn't initially seem as though it would be a problem. Immediately beforehand, Susanna sent what we naively believed to be the final design to the project co-ordinators.

By the time worries had been expressed about the content of the label (something to do with respecting the sensitivity of Latvians – don't ask; it'd take too long to explain), one half of our team was sunning himself on the Costa del Sol.

After making many long-distance phone calls – and sending enough text messages to ensure that we can now do press-ups using only our thumbs – the wrinkles were finally ironed out.

Alas, we tried the patience of St Jamie and St Damian at 26 and St Pom at Cyan Books by sending them this journal entry so late in the day that the 11th hour had to be coerced into accommodating a 61st minute.

Thanks, chaps. You'll all be needing a wee dram, we suspect.

REMOVES STUBBORN LIMESCALE

CHEAP INDUSTRIAL COOKING WHISKY

This is actually an exquisite Scotch malt. It has a slight mustiness and saltiness, together with a lip-smacking combination of Jamaican ginger cake and honeyed malt beer. So we thought you'd appreciate us deterring your guests from trying it. Simply place the bottle on a shelf sufficiently high that they're only able to read the large type. Slàinte!

Single Cask Scotch Malt Whisky
Cask no. 53.92   Aged in oak 25 years
Vol 59.1%   Contents by vol 50cl ℮
Bottled by The Scotch Malt Whisky Society. Produced in Scotland.

26

CASK NUMBER

66.19

Elspeth Murray "Versatile versemonger and weaver of text styles". Among other interesting collaborations Elspeth is poet-in-residence at Glasgow Fort shopping centre, and is writing a play for Reeling and Writhing Theatre Company to tour Scotland in Spring 2006. Iain Valentine Born in 1975, Iain hails from Forfar in Angus (Scotland). He studied at Duncan of Jordanstone College of Art, Dundee, and graduated 1st class BDES (Hons) in Graphic Design & Typography. Previously with Lackie Newton and Navyblue, he is currently design director at Whitespace, Edinburgh.

A SPIRITUAL EXPERIENCE

So where did your ideas come from?

Divine inspiration! There we were, tasting our whisky at the dining room table, when we had a sort of visitation – we saw the light!

What, like the road to Damascus?

Not quite. The glow from a lamp shone through the tasting glass and revealed unto us the shape of a golden angel on a pad of paper.

So that was you all set then?

Not really, because we carried on tasting and wondering about the radiant straw-like colour, the light, airy fragrance, the comforting, approachable feel, the taste – the taste ... as if it were ...

Oh go on, let's have the novice tasters' metaphors.

If this whisky were a book, it would be well-thumbed and full of delicious pudding recipes. If it were a delicious pudding it would be a lemon tart with a blob of cream and a sprig of mint. If it were a garment it would be a favourite corduroy jacket, velvety smooth at the elbows ... And so on.

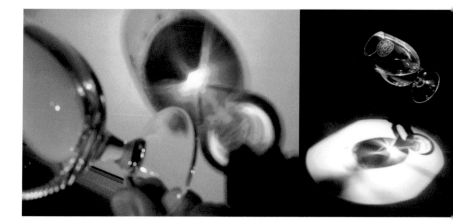

No doubt Iain had some lovely design ideas then.
Absolutely — cosy knits, fluffy baffies, a fireside pipe … and the angel.

So that's what you chose?
Naturellement. Airy, radiant and comforting. Although it took a lot of effort on Iain's part, with help from Niall Hendry, to photograph the angel shape in the studio. And then we found it only worked with The Scotch Malt Whisky Society's own tasting glasses. Here's a photo of the early at-home effort and the more sophisticated set-up with clamps and all. The effect of the light is remarkable and capturing it as an image was an exercise in subtlety.

And what about the words?
At our third meeting, this time at 28 Queen Street, I suggested using a circle poem for the angel's halo. I like the simplicity of this format and the way one can start or stop reading the poem at different points on the circle. And tipping up the bottle to pour a dram lets you see the words from different angles anyway. After our meeting I shredded some pieces of paper and played around with grammatically multi-functional words.

Pardon?

Well, "share" is not only a noun but a verb, for example. And "light" goes one better and triples up as an adjective. These are the kind of words one must round up (sorry!) and employ in a circle poem.

OK. Is that the end of the English language lesson?

Yes. Now onto Scripture Knowledge. For the second part of the text, I used an online concordance of the King James Bible to look up such words as "angel", "drink", "taste", and "smell". By the way, nothing in the authorised version is described as "angelic". The text also sounded more biblical with the removal of excess adjectives. It's just not God's style, apparently.

And the cheeky little "Amen"?

That was Iain's idea. Designers can do words too, you know.

Any other blurring of interdisciplinary boundaries?

Funnily enough, yes and no. I worked up some examples of the text for the circle poem by hand. Iain concedes that my wonky early attempt has more charm than the more precise version but neither made it onto the label.

Clash of the Creatives, was it?

More a case of the limited space – and my respect for Iain's superior graphic experience. Anyway, the poem had gained a word or two by then and I wasn't about to go back to the drawing board and squeeze in "angels" if I didn't have to. Having written the words, I was more than happy to leave the design to Iain. We're both pleased with the label and really enjoyed working together.

So the inspiration was more mutual than divine?

Perhaps the angels had a share in it. Who knows?

MY ANGELS SHARE

THIS ONE SWEET SPIRIT

And I shall place before thee a drink offering, the smell of which is like unto green leaves, and the taste thereof as enfolding arms.

Single Cask Scotch Malt Whisky
Cask No 66.19 Aged in Oak 20 yrs
Produced in Scotland and bottled by
The Scotch Malt Whisky Society – Amen

Vol 54.1% Contents by vol 50cle

26

MALTS

CASK NUMBER

77.11

John Ormston A copywriter, John emigrated from Manchester, near Urmston, in 1984 to escape people's perpetual confusion of his surname. In 2002, he co-founded Henzteeths: a rare breed of writers and now lives in Gullane, East Lothian, 12 miles from Ormiston. **Mark Noë** Mark set up Third Eye Design in 1995. Since then it has consistently been one of the top five design agencies in Scotland. Third Eye's branding work now includes clients such as The Royal Bank of Scotland, University of Kent, Glasgow School of Art, BT, Kshocolat, Mackintosh, Arts & Business and RMJM.

TOTALLY TROPICAL

In the beginning... a summer's afternoon, spent sampling some of the Society's finest whiskies in the company of the great and the good from Scotland's design and writing communities. Cheeks redden and pressures slide as we learn about (or should that be rediscover) the fine art of tasting whisky. Look, smell, taste, feel. First a Lowland; then a Speyside; and then over the sea to Skye. Not a bad way to spend the day.

Oh, the anticipation – the samples are on their way. Emails start circulating with promises of imminent delivery, but still the letterbox stays stubbornly shut ... until, finally, the package arrives. Tightly bound in cream manila; the reassuring "give" of bubble wrap; and, when tilted, the tantalising slosh of something liquid inside. Will I open it now or prolong the anticipation? This must be a little like tantric sex.

A meeting of mouths – diaries synchronised, a meeting in Queen Street's Members' Room is hastily arranged. He'll be wearing an eager expression; I'll be carrying the holy grail (still intact). Smuggling it in past the "Mobiles verboten" sign, up a flight of stairs, then a furtive glance through a doorway to see if we're one or two.

The stage is set: coffee (that can't be right) and water at the ready, the package is carefully unraveled. "Duty free sample for John Ormston

& Mark Noë. Distillery: 77. Sample No: 15." Flushing thoughts of other, lightly coloured samples from our minds, we twist off the cap and neck the contents in one. As if! Though it might have been fun.

Equal measures poured, we stumble forward on our tasting journey. It's pale, very pale – there's consensus on that at least. Very aromatic too. Hints of caramel and fruitcake, liquorice, mango, strawberries and … banana? Thoughts turn to exotic bananaberries and peelable strawberries. The conversation becomes more animated, which draws the barman across to ask for a little "discretion". Duly chastised, we fall to musing on other creative routes. Leaving nothing in the bottle other than a whiff, which I breathe in now as I write this journal, we agree to "have some thoughts" and speak again soon.

Decisions, decisions – the creative juices have been flowing. So far, we've got six concepts on the table: 1) "77" – using the number as a graphic element and type to convey the opposites in the whisky we tasted, supported by a tasting story; 2) "totally tropical man" – using Caribbean-influenced graphics and "taste of the summer" words to create a slightly tongue in cheek label for this perfect summer whisky; 3) "opposites attract" – using mismatched bands of colour and words to show the variety of flavours, i.e. banana on red; 4) "sample" – doing the label like a sample jar or medicine bottle, complete with ingredients and drinking instructions; 5) "tasting wheel" – reproducing the Society's own descriptors, highlighting the ones that we feel are appropriate and handwriting others on top; and 6) "O" – based on the distillery's history and location.

After exploring these further, we agree that the colours/taste experience is definitely the strongest and most true to our tasting session. Instead of writing the flavours on the colours though, we think the colours work stronger on their own. We'll add the tasting notes at the bottom, to make some sense of our ramblings.

And relax... a *fait accompli* (and very nearly to deadline). The label sits centre screen on our respective Mac and laptop. A riot of colour jam-packed with flavour. Crafted, calibrated and kerned to perfection, "Totally Tropical" is ready for public consumption. Just time for a moment's reflection, then back to the keyboard. A journal beckons ...

POP A STRAWBERRY UP YOUR NOSE. PEEL BACK
A BANANA – ONE, TWO, THREE, FOUR. PINEAPPLE
CHUNKS? A SQUARE OF CHOCOLATE, MELTING
IN THE MOUTH. **COCONUT** SHAVINGS. MELTING
PAPAYA AND FRAGRANT MANGO, LACED WITH JET
BLACK   SPICE. DISSOLVES INTO MELTED ICE
CREAM ON THE TONGUE.

Cask no. 77.11
Aged in oak 17yrs
Single Cask Scotch Malt Whisky
Bottled by the Scotch Malt Whisky Society
Produced in Scotland

58.7% Vol

77

26

MALTS

CASK NUMBER

45.16

Donny O'Rourke A graduate of the universities of Glasgow and Cambridge, author or editor of more than a dozen books, Donny has had overlapping careers as poet, television executive, broadcaster, journalist and academic. His latest collection is just out in English and German. Davinder Samrai Davinder is an honours graduate from Glasgow School of Art. After several years as head of design at The Bridge, one of Scotland's leading advertising agencies, he launched Freight in 2001. The consultancy allows him to work across different media including design for print, television graphics, new media and 3-D.

DONNY'S JOURNAL

We sample headingly contrasting drams, the Leith sunshine pouring through the blinds. "My" designer is Davinder, a graphics heavy-hitter and clearly delightful bloke, like me, based in Glasgow. But he doesn't drink whisky. Initially I think this is maybe a wee bit odd, like getting a vegetarian to write about rare steak, but hey why not. Presumably he'll cut out the middle man – i.e. the whisky and either take his cue from me, or dream something up in the abstract. I have never smoked but I could and would attempt a poem about cigarettes.

The whisky arrives, literally, as I am about to walk through the door for a month in Germany and the Czech Republic. I do the ritual smell, swirl, taste, dilute, swirl, taste again, thing and make some (mental) notes. Think about taking bottle with me but customs would have a fit, it is dark and mysterious, it could be anything, a weapon in the war on behalf of terrorism, something really lethal like ... cask strength scotch (a word by the way, we Scots never use ...) I take another thoughtful swiggette, coating my tastebuds with molten gold. I like a drink; but at 10.00am. Suddenly a slope – slippery too.

Dav and I are destined never to meet; the deadlines have been foreshortened, and I am up to my oxters in German poetry (and beer and wine and sausages and ...). Chiding yet patient e-missives arrive. Where is the promised stimulus? Even if he wanted to my design partner can't hit the bottle. Guilt, shame, embarrassment and self-loathing jostle for space in my fretful dreams. Something comes to me about a fire made from sea-weedy beachcombed fish-boxes and west coast sunsets and dried heather in a honey jar and brown water over greybluegreengrey pebbles and glass catching the light of bottle shards. This would be fine if "our" malt was an Islay ...

In Mittel-Europa, I write a poem about Mittel-Europa, a piece about the idea of trying to capture that culture in a whisky glass – convenient, but sincere. Dav will never know; perhaps others will savour and toast and sip and think yeeeeeessss? Berlin with a hint of Budapest: Prague, shot through with Vienna; Krakow and Trieste mingling with Lubljana. Upon my return Dav comes up with his (beautiful) concept. I raise a glass to him. Slàinte. I'm drinking alone.

January star

A Middle-European poet, letting time pass
conceived of "café culture" captured in a glass:
the frivolous and the serious – each sort of Strauss-
Ja, Johann and Richard, in *this* coffee-house
perfumed tobacco, the black Balkan sort,
honeyed hazelnut paste in the apricot torte –
the papers on rods, smelling still of hot type
A kultur on the cusp of rotten and ripe.
Affairs of state, affairs of the heart,
that boy's intrigue with the countess near its end or its start?
The wood polish and oil smell of a Viennese tram …

… Will all be released when you water your dram,
first sip, summer sunset, warm, golden, sehr klar,
silver next, pale and cool as a January star,
a lover's light knock, no battering ram
or so says the flaneur in his dilettante dwam.

DAVINDER'S JOURNAL

Day 1 Donny is missing. I've not even seen the whisky sample. Things aren't going as planned …

Day 3 Geography conspires to keep us apart. I'm in Glasgow, Donny is in Germany. He goes to the Highlands; I'm in Sicily!

We converse via email. The banter is great but I'm conscious that we're yet to make any tangible headway.

Day 7 An email arrives; Donny tells me about the direction his thoughts are moving. I am a grateful recipient – as I'm doing everything I promised I wouldn't – exploring stylistic treatments in the absence of actual content.

Day 9 Our relationship is almost a tease. There is always the promise of more from both sides – although neither of us knows how it will manifest itself. I don't know what Donny wants from me and I suspect he's thinking the same.

Day 14 Donny's finished piece arrives to a rousing silent applause. (No one knows what I'm working on – I've been keeping it a secret.) Don't know why I like it but I do. The poem is powerful. The whisky was obviously very potent.

Day 16 I'm "tasting" the whisky by remote, but strangely it's an entirely satisfying experience. Donny is living up to his reputation. His words have struck a chord ...

Two lines sing out:

"Affairs of state, affairs of the heart, that boy's intrigue with the countess near its end or its start?"

A bolt of lightening and I'm being taken on a new journey.

To me, the words evoke almost a sexual awakening. I envisage a boy spying on the source of his obsession ... a peek-a-boo type relationship.

I'd argue it almost mirrors Donny and me (without the sexual element!).

A whirlwind of activity and I think I'm there.

All is NOT revealed in the final design. Maybe Donny and I were holding back ... ?

A success? I think so. I hope Donny agrees.

**SINGLE CASK
SCOTCH MALT
WHISKY**

CASK NO
45.16

AGED IN OAK
29 YRS

VOL
50cl

VOL
49.2%

AFFAIRS OF STATE, AFFAIRS OF THE HEART,
THAT BOY'S INTRIGUE WITH THE COUNTESS
NEAR ITS END OR ITS START?

BOTTLED BY THE SCOTCH MALT WHISKY SOCIETY
PRODUCED IN SCOTLAND

26 MALTS

CASK NUMBER

37.27

Kate Patrick Kate, 39, usually produces her best work at the last minute, under the pressure of a tight deadline: this includes writing articles for newspapers and magazines, ironing cricket whites, sewing elastic on ballet shoes, creating witch make-up and pulling off an authentic mushroom risotto for eight guests. Ron Burnett With over thirty years' experience, Ron's career spans teaching, publishing, corporate and brand design for both the public and private sectors. A malt whisky "enthusiast", his particular expertise lies in designing successful branding and packaging for many major spirits producers.

KATE'S JOURNAL

The journey to *A Lover's Lassie*

The whisky sample arrives, with broken lid. Does this mean it will evaporate before my eyes?

Ron, my designer partner, is up to his eyes in work, and has sent me the most convoluted instructions as to how to find his office — it will be amazing if I don't end up in one of the haunted underground vaults beneath the Royal Mile.

I love our whisky; it's like opening up a box of ripe, succulent fruit; the barley is there too, and the colour is like riverbank marigold, with absolutely brilliant clarity.

A sunny morning, Friday 13th. I'm driving the wrong way up the Royal Mile because I missed the turn to Ron's wyndy fastness. It turns out his directions were immaculate; I just needed to have followed them. Eventually I find him, tucked away at the back of the Canongate in some pretty interesting premises. We go to his "east wing" — a meeting room displaying whiskies for which he's previously created the labels.

And here's the rub. Ron and I both know a bit about whisky. Just enough to be dangerous. He's used to creating identities for brands in an utterly commercial context. He usually knows every minute detail about who it's aimed at and what the "story" is. So it's hard for him to be working with anonymity like this. I know a bit, through my husband having been in the trade for 12 years, from my writing and because I have developed, gradually, my own taste for discovering what's in the spectrum of malt whisky. We really shouldn't get this horribly wrong. But we're both a bit afraid we might.

It's only a few minutes before our whisky becomes a persona. She's a woman; blonde; about 20, slightly experienced and therefore "up" for it; spring-like, yet surrounded by ripe fruit; not an earth mother, yet with a sparky warmth.

Ron suggests we view her as Botticelli's *Birth of Venus* – but rising not from an oyster shell, rather from a basket of fruit and barley. The message is clear: this whisky is pure nature, little affected by the cask, still with the aroma of the countryside from which it was distilled. I think our lassie should be holding a pear: this is our overwhelming impression. Peardrops, from childhood sweetie shops.

To anchor her to Scotland, it will not be a mini kilt, but a purple landscape behind. She is close to nature, this female; but she is essentially "together", and knowing what she wants: she wants her lover to come and get her. She is, in fact, her lover's lassie.

I'm off to do some words; Ron's going to organise an illustration. It'll be an illustratively-led label, but with some interesting typography too. Unashamedly romantic, floral, like the flower fairies books. We may even include some love cherubs. No room for contemporary minimalism in this concept.

As luck would have it, Ron's wife, Jacqueline, is a professional artist, so he gives her our brief and she produces the stunning image before us. It is a little too briny at first go: we want a hint of river, mountain and waterfall, but essentially the message is to fuse youth, perfect form, meadow and fruit. She is also a little too blonde for my liking: the whisky may have clarity, but she's no Essex girl.

A few days, a few emails later, I have nailed down the words and Ron the typeface. He suggests things to me; I suggest back. It's very amicable and relaxed. We are both mischievously happy with the final product of our crazy, creative fling.

RON'S JOURNAL

Day 1: Email invitation to participate in project. Great feeling to be involved; wanted; considered; loved; rated!

Day 2: Receipt of brief. Good … but not sure who I'm paired with; don't know all the names of writers and designers. Grave concerns about the total "freedom" of the brief, being so used to working for the spirits industry within the confines of brand identity, positioning, markets, marketeers, etc. Also really concerned about fitting this in with my workload.

Day 3: SMWS tasting. Briefing from SMWS people, interesting, although as an existing member, know a little about tasting procedure and

language although by no means any kind of tasting expert. Amazed by number of creatives there I didn't know. Shame that Kate, my writer partner couldn't make it.

Day 4: The start of the creative bit. Met up with Kate for the first time. Lovely person, first time we'd worked together. She had our tasting sample ... assume designers could not be entrusted with an alcoholic sample! Spent an hour and a half nosing/tasting/brainstorming/ doodling. Easy. Both on same wavelength, similar reactions to taste, etc., agreed pretty quickly where we were going ... in short, create a character out of its personality. Need illustrator to realise our idea. Kate to go and finalise words. Relief and elation at how well this is working.

Day 5: Brief my painter wife Jacqueline Watt to illustrate our idea.

Day 6: Kate sends me words. Really good, a beautiful interpretation of our ideas and Jacqueline produces smashing illustration. I put typography and image together into various design layouts. Struggle a bit fitting the words into the illustration. Not happy with it.

Day 7: Revise the layout. A couple of options begin to work. Send to Kate who corrects my punctuation! Agree on changes to illustration and submit our preferred version as it stands as a visual.

Day 8: Positive response from SMWS and 26. Some mutterings about us recreating a Botticelli ... if only we were that blinkin' good!

Day 9: Get new revised illustration (tweaks more than anything else). Looks really good. Incorporate into artwork.

Day 10: Send to Kate for final "sign-off". Send to SMWS. Damned good if I say so myself. Finished. Hurrah. Await the exhibition!

A Lover's Lassie ~

From nature's | her freshness has
fruitful basket,   caught the
a sweet peardrop.   attention
Perfectly   of an
formed   admirer.
beauty,   A knowing
with smooth,   gaze; a
barley-gold   harmonious
locks.   future.

SINGLE CASK SCOTCH MALT WHISKY

Cask Nr. 37.27

Aged in Oak 19 Years

BOTTLED BY THE
SCOTCH MALT WHISKY SOCIETY   Contents by Vol. 50cle
PRODUCED IN SCOTLAND
                              Vol. 59.6%

26

MALTS

CASK NUMBER

27.60

Sara Sheridan Sara is a novelist, copywriter and journalist. She recently won a Sky Movies Max award for her short film *The Window Bed* and is currently working on an historical novel set in China after the Opium War. She lives in Edinburgh. David Freer David was a student in Glasgow and Rhode Island. He started his career at Saatchi & Saatchi in crutches because of a fall from Glasgow's infamous Duke of Wellington statue. His toilet signs are used in Jamie Oliver's 15 restaurant.

SARA'S JOURNAL

The rules of this game are different. We don't have to sell anything. Not in the way we do in the normal run of things. That makes it Art. We fumble and flutter in our working lives between Art and Money. Personally I am in favour of both.

David and I are different too. We realise this when we meet for the first time in Borders in Glasgow. His world is visual, he loves the countryside, he likes whisky and is about to get married. My world is conceptual, I have just slabbed my entire garden, have big plans for being an old maid and rarely drink alcohol.

However we both seem to like playing games and over the weeks we have plenty of chances for that. Guessing who at the whisky tasting is a designer, who is a writer. Guessing where they're from. Blind tasting our whisky and naming its equivalent in the world of fashion and film. Our whisky, for the avoidance of doubt, is Steve McQueen. Our whisky is Issey Miyake. A connoisseur's tipple. A purist's dram with a twist of originality.

It came in the post in a small, flat bottle. It was a disturbingly pale yellow and we were worried it looked a bit on the medical side. We reckoned we better sniff it first. We met at the Society's rooms in Queen Street to taste it together. At first, we had a few clever ideas in the abstract. Edgy, arty stuff of course, but when we downed the first mouthful we realised it didn't suit this whisky. Like anything of true quality it was about its own experience. This is interesting because in the advertising industry, where we both work, we spend a lot of time broadening the experience of products. When you are selling things they often become about their associated experiences. About lifestyle and benefits. Buy this chocolate bar and you will become a skateboarding hero or buy this house and domestic bliss will be yours. But of course, we weren't selling.

However, we realised, second dram down, that we were in competition, and that competition was blind. We had no idea what the other twenty-five teams were going to get up to. Would all twenty-six of us come up with the same thing? This would make the project an artwork of a different calibre. A collection of twenty-six bottles, identical and yet each with a different creative team behind them. That, we decided, could go into the Tate.

For a while we played Guess What Everyone Else Is Doing and then realised that in fact there was a strange feeling of insecurity in not knowing. What if our bottle was, well, pants compared to everyone else's? What if we were up against twenty-five teams of creative genius and it turned out that we were only middling?

Thank heavens we liked our whisky. Even I liked it. Small sip after small sip it grew on me. It was devoid of frivolity. It had no gimmicks, no easy way in. With powerful directness it simply said Drink Me.

We loved Drink Me. It reminded us of Alice in Wonderland, of course. But it also tied in with the uncompromising nature of the product. Then David had the idea of making a black and white photograph. A plate, hand printed. Something of a similar quality to the whisky itself. The best of its kind. A classic. We hit on the idea of an empty glass. An empty glass on the front of a full bottle. We liked that and decided it had to be grainy and handmade and rough round the edges. Very old school. The real McCoy. I scribbled a poem in my notebook, an obdurate sexual come-on based around drink me. A love line from the whisky to the drinker. In the end we didn't use it though, we decided we didn't need to. Drink me would be enough.

David found a fantastic, traditional photographer in Glasgow called Jamie Maitland. We met in a bar near Queen Street station and he sipped the whisky furtively, stretching our small sample to its limits. We decided on no enhanced images, nothing fake, just a really good photograph with no frills. David had matched the colour of the whisky on his pantone chart. We decided that a white label would look cheap against the tone of the liquid and played around with different shades of pale yellow, finding one we liked.

It was surprisingly easy. "Do tell us all your artistic differences in the journal," they said. But we didn't have any. There really wasn't much to fight about.

Jamie produced a great image. He works from home and, having supplied a couple of Scotch Malt Whisky Society glasses, he got to work in his darkroom. Crystal it turned out photographed better than glass. Then we wanted a rough-edged print but when he phoned around to find the right transparency holder all the Glasgow shops were out of stock. Edinburgh too. There had been a mysterious and sudden rush and no hope of anything less than a two-week delivery whereas we had to deliver the design in two days. We were panicked, flapping around, when David sat down on top of a CD case which, he realised, was more or less the same size as what we needed. After an hour Jamie had made it up by hand, masked with duct tape and filed down at the edges. In the end we had prints the same day, which was amazing. And as we had vowed not to digitally retouch anything, any small changes had to be done by hand, the good old-fashioned way, in the darkroom.

In a way, though, this is only half the experience. We loved producing the label but the really interesting thing will be seeing it lined up with the other twenty-five. So Slan, enjoy the dram that says DRINK ME.

drink me

Cask No. 27.60
Single Cask Scotch Malt Whisky
Aged in oak 15 years
Produced in Scotland
Bottled by The Scotch Malt Whisky Society

Contents by vol 50cl e   Vol 54.9%

26

CASK NUMBER

26.40

John Simmons John is a writer, consultant and founding director of 26. He is writer-in-chief at *www.thewriter.co.uk* and has worked with many major brands on tone of voice. His most recent book is *Dark Angels: How writing releases creativity at work.* Harry Pearce Harry's work has won awards worldwide, including silver D&ADs. He was one of a few graphic designers chosen for a show of excellence in NYC, and had work exhibited at the 50th anniversary of the Alliance Graphique Internationale, Paris. He sits on the WITNESS Advisory Board, a human rights organisation in NYC.

When the whisky arrived I unwrapped it as if I had been sent a precious archaeological find. Inside the bubble wrap was a sample bottle looking like, well, a sample bottle. If I had taken it to my GP for analysis he might have discovered an excess of alcohol, a remarkable 50+%, and given me a quizzical look.

However, I met Harry Pearce my design partner at the Society rooms in Bleeding Heart Yard. It was strange that our distillery number was 26 which I traced on a map to the northern Highlands, further north than I'd ever been in Britain. The helpful manager suggested that the distillery was Clynlish.

Harry and I started nosing and tasting. Our conversation seemed to revolve around mysteries, philosophy and riddles, no doubt because malt whisky is something of a puzzle to us. We talked about the Sphinx and elixirs before moving on to alchemy. Perhaps this was triggered too by the golden glow of the sun through the whisky in our glasses. But there are mysteries and mysteries. Both of us are defiant refusers of the *Da Vinci Code* (perhaps we'll be the only two people left in the country not to have read it?). It might be because it's badly written or because, as Harry puts it "it's stolen from a far greater mystery, but we're wide open to the journey of true mysteries". There is something appropriate in trying to unlock the code to describe the mystery of making malt whisky. From simple raw materials like barley and water, this golden liquid is created through a kind of alchemy.

▽ & — over ☾,
⊕ gleam, changes over ♃
To a ⊙ ☿.
As above so below.

We carried on tasting. Was there a little hint of iron in there, a metal? The taste was like water flowing over a stone, dappled and gilded with sunlight. We talked about the philosopher's stone and Harry was much more expert than I. He had a book called *The Philosopher's Stone* that he would share with me; he offered to send it to me so I could read it while in Greece on holiday. He was interested in alchemy's use of symbols, as well as its history and philosophy. He convinced me that there was more to it than avaricious men trying to become rich through turning base metals into gold. And he discovered a sixteenth century quotation about the "drinkable gold of eternal youth".

There was a magic too in 26, the number of our distillery and the title of our group, named after the letters in the alphabet. I wondered about writing a poem, perhaps of 26 words or 26 syllables. If I wrote such a poem could words be replaced by alchemical symbols to create a code? What would be the words that remained? Harry talked about phrases from alchemy like "As above so below" and "All is one and one is all". As we sat there, glasses in hand, it seemed that drinking whisky – the act of smelling, tasting, savouring – related to reflection, meditation, philosophy. Perhaps our label should aid the reflective process, going with the grain of whisky drinking, and give drinkers something to ponder as they drank, to meditate on some mysteries of life as true alchemists might have done. For the purposes of this meditation, whisky's true essence was the metaphorical gold we sought.

We went our ways. Harry sent me Peter Marshall's book *The Philosopher's Stone*, and I read this about alchemy:

"First and foremost, alchemy is the art and science of transformation. It is an ancient body of beliefs and practices which seeks to transmute base metal into gold and produce an elixir to prolong life."

I read too that Michael Scotus was magus and would-be alchemist at the court of Frederick II, Emperor of the Romans. "Scotus" was a description of his Scottishness, a distinctive identity label in thirteenth century Italy. It meant that there was a Scottish association with

alchemy. It also reminded me of a poem by Gerard Manley Hopkins called *Duns Scotus's Oxford*, and I was interested in the poetic sound and compressed language of Hopkins for my own poem.

Away for a week in Greece, I thought about alchemy and whisky, then I wrote this poem:

> Water flow over stone,
> Barley gleam, changes over time
> To a gold glow.
> As above so below.
>
> The life root under earth,
> Peat fire, forges sun metal
> From its wood shoot.
> As within so without.
>
> When tides pull beneath the moon
> I am its reflection, the light
> In quest of the eternal.
> All is one and one is all.

Here we have 26 ingredient words that can be said to symbolise the alchemy that lies in the making of this whisky. What remains when these words are taken out as symbols, the essence that is distilled, are the phrases of alchemy that contain neither material noun nor active verb. These are the only words left on the label, the apparent truths that reveal the presence of a code. What you are left with is contained inside the bottle: look at this whisky when it is shot through with the light of the sun or by night with the glow of an open fire. It is gold, more golden than gold itself.

I decided that the words that could be symbolised should primarily be nouns. But nouns cannot live alone, they need the support of verbs to give them meaning. Yet there are nouns that become verbs without changing a single letter – they transmute from noun to verb and back again as if by alchemy. These were the substantial words that formed the ingredients of the poem, the ingredients to describe the alchemy of whisky-making.

Harry was excited by these explorations too. He set to work researching the symbols of alchemy and discovered enough genuine alchemical symbols to replace words and give the label enough sense of mystery. There are 26 alchemical ingredients shown by 26 words and symbols that form the spine of a poem. Perhaps influenced by my holiday in Greece, where I had visited the Mycenean sites, I considered it the Linear B language of whisky-making. It has the appearance of an alchemical riddle, a mystery that has its own code, but it can be deciphered by those prepared to indulge it with time and reflection.

Other wonders emerged from the research and informed Harry's design. The alchemical symbol for gold is a perfect circle with a dot in its centre. The circle seemed to reflect the alchemist's philosophy set out in the poem. *As above, so below:* it has perfect symmetry. *As within so without:* the outer and inner circles are the same but of different sizes. *All is one and one is all:* the circle expresses wholeness. But also a bold graphic mark, a focal point and, we guessed, a counterpoint to some of the other label approaches. A modernist statement of ancient wisdom, its black and whiteness allowing the gold of the whisky to be the only colour.

So here was our elixir made in a distillery numbered 26. The process had transformed water, yeast and barley into the glowing gold of this malt whisky, a whisky that might do wondrous things for you. At the very least it will allow you to reflect and wonder.

i gleam, changes over ♃
To a ☉ ☽.
As above so below.

The ♀ ☌ under ♀,
Peat △, ⚹ ☉ metal
From its ▽ shoot.
As within so without.

When ⌒ pull beneath the ☽
I am its ↗, the light
In ✢ of the ☆,
All is one and one is all.

Bottled by
The Scotch
Malt Whisky Society

26MALTS

CASK NUMBER
26.42

Neil Urquhart Neil joined The Big Picture as creative director in 2004. A freelance writer for 12 years, he gave it all up for the chance to work on spirit accounts such as Rémy Martin and The Macallan. No fool then. Paul Sudron Having already worked in Edinburgh for over 10 years, Paul joined Elmwood in February 2002 as design director. His passions include Middlesbrough Football Club ("The Boro") and a keen interest in Garden Sheds.

HINTS OF WHAT HAPPENED
A journal of long distance collaboration

Colour

NU: Travel down to Edinburgh for whisky tasting in the George Street premises of The Scotch Malt Whisky Society. Tasting is interesting. Learn all about tears, legs and church windows. Learn nothing about Paul. He's not there.

PS: Before the project started what I knew about malt whisky could have been typed 12 point on a postage stamp. When I did finally make a tasting, I learnt a lot about the "process" of whisky making, although it took a good week before I regained the full use of my taste buds.

NU: The whisky sample arrives by courier one Friday evening. Unfortunately friends also arrive from Glasgow to stay the weekend. The sample is small with flecks of charcoal. The friends are curious and persistent. Predictably, we drink the sample. Not much to begin with, but very little left now. On a positive note – we all loved the whisky.

Discover on the Monday morning that the sample is supposed to be shared with design partner. Email an apology and send remaining drop to Paul in Edinburgh.

A WEE SENSATION

PS: I'm expecting a full 75cl bottle through the post to savour – only to be greeted by a thimbleful in a medicine bottle with brown bits floating in it!

Taste
PS: Call Neil to discuss project. Decline the offer of a new sample. Suggest that the label should be typographically led, possibly focused on the words describing the colour, aroma and flavour. Also suggest that we keep clear of traditional whisky imagery. It's a taste thing.

NU: Like Paul's ideas for the label – but not so sure about focusing on the aroma and taste words. In an email, explain how personally the whole thing about "hints of cold wood ash and ham baked in foil" leaves me scratching my head.

For me drinking whisky is much more about the emotional experience – "hints of laughter and friendship" and I would like to see a label reflect this. Suggest that the label carries a very short story based on an emotional experience. I have in my mind an old crofter I once knew who would always call a dram a "wee sensation".

PS: Receive first draft from Neil. Like the idea of presenting a short story on the label. Create a number of initial designs. Steer clear of scripty fonts and use colours that hint at the subject matter, but with a modern twist. My favourite is where the type is split one word per line.

NU: I love the colour themes and I like the visual impact of Paul's one word per line designs, but I don't think it works with every part of the story. It's too staccato. Loses the flow, loses the emotion.

PS: Feedback from Neil. Have a little tinker with the copy and bring things closer together. Work with the font for the opening few words – it's Clarendon – but I take a couple of photocopies and distress small areas just to give it a bit more personality.

NU: More emails. Looking for the right emphasis.

PS: More changes. Looking for the right balance.

NU: More tweaks.

PS: More PDFs.

Finish
PS:Final alts and our design is submitted.

Turn our attention to the journal. Suggest a good point to make would be that while the words and design came together, the two of us never actually met, and our collaboration was all long distance.

NU: Long or short – it worked – and now it's finished.

Hints of smoke,
cold wood ash
and antiseptic.

That was Ian.

And that's your
DRAM he'd say.

A
WEE
SENSATION

Good times.

A house in
the hills,
an old crofter
and friends.

The aftertaste
is lingering
and strong.

A drop of water;
wipe my eyes and
taste the salt.

Traces of
laughter and
collie dogs.

Now
before
you
go,
you'll
be
having
another.

One more.

A WEE
SENSATION

SINGLE CASK
SCOTCH MALT WHISKY.
CASK No. 26.42
AGED 12 YEARS

BOTTLED BY
THE SCOTCH MALT WHISKY SOCIETY.
PRODUCED IN SCOTLAND

#26

VOLUME:
58.5%

CONTENTS BY:
50cl e

ABOUT 26

26 is a national organisation dedicated to championing the creative use of language in business. Its members are made up of writers, designers, language specialists and communications and marketing professionals. 26 holds talks, readings and seminars and has initiated three large-scale creative projects linking writers and designers. *26 Letters: Illuminating the Alphabet* brought 26 writers together with 26 designers to create a poster for each letter of the alphabet for an exhibition at The British Library as part of the 2004 London Design Festival. *From Here to Here* is a creative collaboration between London Underground, students from London College of Communications and writers from 26 based on the Circle Line and will result in an exhibition at the 2005 London Design Festival. *26 Malts* will also be part of the 2005 London Design Festival having first been on show at The Scotch Malt Whisky Society, 28 Queen Street, Edinburgh, during August 2005.

www.26.org.uk

ABOUT THE SCOTCH MALT WHISKY SOCIETY

The Scotch Malt Whisky Society began life some twenty years ago when a group of friends shared the price of a cask of fine malt whisky. Today the Society remains true to its origins retaining its personal and companionable atmosphere with three superb venues and over 27,000 members worldwide.

The Society selects casks from distilleries the length and breadth of Scotland and sometimes elsewhere. The whiskies are only available to members and every whisky selected and bottled by the Society has been tasted, discussed and scored by the Tasting Panel. This essential process ensures that the Society selects whiskies that appeal to members' enthusiasm for quality, variety, interest and their sense of adventure!

Through the Panel, a unique Tasting Note is created for each malt by delving deep to find verbal metaphors and analogies. The tasting notes entertain and provoke as well as inform. The Society conducts whisky tastings and events all around the world.

Relaxed, involving and above all enjoyable, there's no better way to discover whisky than The Scotch Malt Whisky Society.

· To become a member of The Scotch Malt Whisky Society go to *www.smws.com* or phone **0131 555 2929** (Mon–Fri 9.00am–4.45pm).

ABOUT ARTS & BUSINESS

A&B

Arts & Business *working together*

Arts & Business aspires to be the world's most successful and widespread creative network. We help business people support the arts and the arts inspire business people, because good business and great art together create a richer society.

Our dual mission is to enable business to be more successful by engaging with the arts, and to increase resources for the arts from business.

We have been the connecting point for the business and arts communities for the past 30 years across the UK, and at the heart of our work is the knowledge that the arts deliver unique, creative solutions that help business to achieve success. That is why we are happy to be supporting this inspiring project with 26 and The Scotch Malt Whisky Society.

At Arts & Business we deliver a full range of programmes and services for both our arts and business members. To find out about what we can do for your organisation, visit our website at: *www.AandB.org.uk*

ABOUT THE LONDON DESIGN FESTIVAL 2005

The London Design Festival is an annual international event established to celebrate and promote London and the UK's creativity. By dedicating the last two weeks in September to design, a diverse range of individuals and organisations are able to come together, celebrate the creative diversity of London, discover new ideas, make new connections, and most importantly, have fun.

The 2005 Festival includes contributions from over 100 partner organisations, from retailers to museums, trade bodies to designer makers. It's an exceptionally busy time of year with exhibitions, showcases, seminars, talks, screenings, and the odd party ...

The Festival is inclusive in its approach to design. An estimated 25 disciplines are represented, from graphic, product, furniture, and fashion design – all of which are well represented alongside interactive design, post-production, architecture, writing and advertising.

London is one of, if not *the* creative capital of the world. The London Design Festival presents a unique opportunity to celebrate and enjoy this fact, alongside people from around the world exploring new ideas, making connections, doing business and enjoying the fruits of their creative pursuits. The London Design Festival 2005 takes place 15–30 September.

www.londondesignfestival.com

WRITERS' AND DESIGNERS' CONTACT DETAILS

Alan Ainsley
alan_c_ainsley@yahoo.co.uk

Chris Allen
chris@designlinks.co.uk

John Allert
John.Allert@interbrand.com

Rob Andrews
rob.andrews@r-d-co.com

Nick Asbury
mail@nickasbury.com

Will Awdry
Will.Awdry@DDBlondon.com

Craig Barnes
digger@madeonceonly.com

Patrick Bergel
patrick@thehorsehospital.com

Alan Black
alan@blackad.co.uk

Ben Braber
benbraber@bbmc.co.uk

Victor Brierley
Victorjtb@aol.com

Ron Burnett
ron@graphicpartners.co.uk

Sarah Burnett
sarah.burnett3@btopenworld.com

Nick Copland
nick.copland@elmwood.co.uk

Ultan Coyle
ultan@good-creative.com

George Craigie
george@designiscrucial.com

Stuart Delves
stuart@henzteeth.com

Matthew Fitt
mjfitt@ntlworld.com

Susanna Freedman
susanna@tsuko.co.uk

David Freer
david@freerdesign.co.uk

Nina Gronblom
nina.gronblom@tayburn.co.uk

Chris Harrison
chris@harrisonandco.com

Roger Horberry
rogerhorberry@hotmail.com

Jules Horne
jules@texthouse.net

Jamie Jauncey
jamie@jauncey.co.uk

Martin Lee
martin.lee@acacia-avenue.com

Karen McCarthy
karen@karenmccarthy.co.uk

Aird McKinstrie
aird@mckinstriewilde.co.uk

Charles MacLean
whiskymac@ednet.co.uk

Richard Medrington
richard@puppetstate.com

Chris Miller
chris@miller.name

Damian Mullan
damian@soitbegins.co.uk

Elspeth Murray
elspeth@elspethmurray.com

Rodney Mylius
rodney.mylius@fortunestreet.com

Mark Noë
mark@thirdeyedesign.co.uk

Donny O'Rourke
donny.orourke@btinternet.com

John Ormston
john@henzteeth.com

Kate Patrick
katepk@blueyonder.co.uk

Harry Pearce
harry.p@lippapearce.com

Prem Reynolds
prem@big-picture.co.uk

Lucy Richards
Lucy@StudioLR.com

Davinder Samrai
DSamrai@freightdesign.co.uk

Jeremy Scholfield
JScholfield@gasoline.uk.com

Graham Scott
graham@nevisdesign.co.uk

Sara Sheridan
sarasheridan@hotmail.com

John Simmons
johnsimmons@blueyonder.co.uk

Paul Sudron
paul.sudron@elmwood.co.uk

John Tafe
John@frontpage.co.uk

Kyn Taylor
kyn.taylor@fortunestreet.com

Gillian Thomas
gt@thepartners.co.uk

Neil Urquhart
neil@big-picture.co.uk

Iain Valentine
iain@whitespacers.com